BEER KITS AND BREWING

VALETE

Tragically, Dave Line died whilst this book was still at the galley-proof stage.

Those who are familiar with his earlier writings on beer making will miss his authority. Those who knew him personally will miss his humour and inventiveness. Those who are about to meet him, through the pages of this book, will realise that they have lost a fine mentor.

This book is his epitaph – the best tribute you can pay to Dave is to brew a better pint for having read it.

March, 1980

Ben Bennetts

DEDICATION
To Sheila and Robert

THANKS
To Sheila for typing the manuscript and to my five year old son Robert, for not helping too much with the brewing experiments!

BEER KITS AND BREWING

Dave Line

BEER KITS AND BREWING
DAVE LINE

Published by:
"The Amateur Winemaker" Publications Ltd.,
South Street, Andover, Hants.
SP10 2BU

1st Impression 1980
2nd Impression 1981
3rd Impression 1984

ISBN 0 900841 59 1

Printed in Great Britain by:
STANDARD PRESS (Andover) Ltd.
South Street, Andover

CONTENTS

CHAPTER 1

INTRODUCING THIS BOOK

"BEER KITS AND BREWING" is a great new book on home brewing packed full of the latest information on equipment, ingredients and techniques and with 50 exciting recipes for you to try. The book concentrates on the practical side of home brewing and tells beermakers here, and the enthusiastic band of followers in North America, how to brew good beer without fuss and complication from these new products.

The ever increasing number of home brewers, satisfied with the first class pints of beer they brew so simply and economically, have rocketed the popularity of the hobby to the country's leading leisure pastime. The boom has led to the trade providing a better service and more reliable products, and this in turn has meant that some of the traditional forms of ingredients and original brewing equipment are no longer available. In the light of these new innovations many of the earlier books on the subject are now obsolete.

In this much-needed up to date book on home brewing, beer kits, hopped worts, barley syrups and the full range of malt extracts are examined frankly, factually and in a logical manner which must appeal to beginner and enthusiast alike. All the popular new pressure barrels, CO_2 gas injector systems, heaters and a whole host of brewing aids are discussed to enable the reader to make a sensible and economic choice of equipment and materials.

For the serious minded brewer, sections are devoted to advanced techniques of mashing and quality control. Such skills are essential for matching the best commercial beers available and for competition work.

The main satisfaction will be in brewing good, wholesome beer. My reward is in knowing you can share the enjoyment I experienced supping a new brew, savouring it and declaring it worthy of inclusion as a recipe. It's a hard life, writing a book on brewing beer!

CHAPTER 2

BEER KITS

Beer kits are the most popular way of brewing beer at home. The quality of the brew can be very good indeed and it has been known for kit beers to win prizes in beer competitions. Ultimately, the conventional do-it-yourself brewing methods using mashing or malt extract will produce the better beer, but kits are an attractive proposition to those who wish to brew beer at home without making too much of a hobby of it. Brewing technique is just as important as being presented with balanced ingredients in a kit and thus the procedures explained later in the book will benefit the user enormously.

What are Beer Kits, then? Basically they are a concentrate of malt and hops and all the home brewer has to do is add water, sugar and yeast to ferment the brew. Beer kits cut out all the preliminary "cooking" stages which can be a very messy business. They eliminate the need for stocking numerous brewing materials and for possessing the knowledge of how to use them. They also cut out the guesswork and the likelihood of failure for the inexperienced user.

Reducing the human element factor in brewing is a big plus in favour of using kits. We "humans" can make an awful mess of a well-meaning malt extract or grain beer recipe. These methods are inherently more complex and thus have more to go wrong if the brewer does not appreciate some of the finer points of the procedure. Easy methods have created the situation where Beer Kit entries often win major show awards in competitions, and this is a real measure of their success.

I have a simple philosophy regarding Beer Kits. If you use Beer Kits and you are happy with the results and economics of the exercise there is no need to read further than this chapter because you have got all the satisfaction home brewers seek. However, the mere fact you are reading this book probably means that you suspect that more could be achieved by collecting and brewing the ingredients yourself. And I couldn't agree more.

Different Types of Kits

There are three main approaches to manufacturing beer kits. The first is the obvious. A beer is produced much in the same way as in a commercial brewery. Malt hops, and grain are boiled together for an hour or so and from the spent solids a *hopped wort* is strained off. In fact many beer kits are by-products from actual breweries and are produced from the same high quality ingredients as for the commercial trade. In a proper brewery, 5 gallons of hopped wort would be required to brew 5 gallons of beer. As such it is a bulky package and would not be a practical proposition for the home brew trade. A beer kit the size of a large suitcase weighing as much as a full pressure barrel could not be described as a convenience product! To overcome this problem, the hopped wort is concentrated until, with most of its water removed, it occupies about one twentieth of its original volume. All the goodness is retained in a small can of manageable proportions.

The second approach is to start with a malt extract base and add the other brewing ingredients as required. From a manufacturing point of view this technique is extremely versatile, making it easy to imitate any style of beer. Hop extract, caramel colouring, yeast nutrient, finings and heading salts can be dosed in with laboratory precision to match exactly the desired beer flavour and character. This brings out an interesting point: I am often asked if it is worth experimenting with beer kits by adding for instance, more hops to increase bitterness or malt extract to achieve a fuller bodied brew. With a few exceptions the answer is an emphatic NO. Do not tamper with beer kits unless you are a very experienced home brewer. The manufacturers spend a lot of effort presenting a *balanced* beer for you to brew and upsetting the precise formulation by adding other ingredients indiscriminately must be doomed to failure. Some beer kits do suggest variations and obviously these are quite valid. Also the modifications I suggest will produce interesting variations, but on the whole if you are not satisfied with a particular kit, change to another or progress to the full do-it-yourself approach that is the main theme of this book.

Finally, there are the beer kits formulated entirely from dry ingredients comprising usually fresh hops, granular malt, dried malt extract powder and yeast. Dry kits have the smallest share of the market and are either designed as economy beers or better quality beers, sometimes employing sophisticated techniques such as mashing.

Allowing the manufacturer to give the exact proportions of all the ingredients needed can be a money saver for the occasional home brewer who brews up only now and again. Under these circumstances buying all the ingredients separately for a do-it-yourself approach could be very wasteful.

Brewing with Kits

The brewing instructions given with each beer kit must cater for the person who is a complete beginner with no previous experience of brewing.

Simplicity is the keyword and fortunately the majority of kits are blessed with decent instructions. Having tried and tested numerous beer kits myself, the main conclusion I came to was that it is essential to follow the instructions as closely and precisely as possible. It is quite remarkable how the quality of the finished beer can be ruined if the instructions are not followed to the letter. Beer kits seem to be more sensitive on this point than other brewing methods.

My experiments with kits have produced some interesting variations. Using a dark sugar such as Demerara, Light Soft Brown or even Golden Syrup produces some luscious flavour tones when substituted for whole or part of the recommended white sugar quota.

Some brews I found to be a bit harsh on the palate when drunk young as suggested in the "Ready in 10 days" recipes. The addition of 3–5 saccharin tablets to the fermenting bin will help smooth out the roughness without imparting a detectable sweetness.

Another common defect is the lack of fresh hop flavour and aroma stemming from the use of isomerised hop extracts in the production stage. Powdering a few pellets of fresh hops into the fermenting bin during the latter stages of fermentation offsets this loss.

I must emphasise again that these modifications may not work with all kits and indeed are not necessary with the majority. They are mainly for the person who is basically pleased with a particular kit but feels the finished beer lacks something in the quarters mentioned.

13

Most beer kits do work out to be slightly more expensive than equivalent flavoured brews produced by the standard malt extract methods. Advocates of kits feel the convenience of the "instant" beer concept to be well worth the extra few pence.

Types of Beer

It is a surprising fact that few beer drinkers can positively identify more than three or four types of beer commercially available. Knowing a bit more about these brews is helpful in selecting a beer kit and becomes essential for the serious brewer who is thinking about entering beers under strict classification in competitions.

The majority of British breweries base their production on two light brews and a dark one. Considering the light brews first, we have ORDINARY BITTER; a fairly low alcohol beverage designed for quick production and quick consumption. It is the drinking man's favourite tipple for quaffing in large quantities over an evening's session. The beer itself is normally a light golden colour, light in body as well. Despite its name, the brew should have a predominate hop *flavour* rather than bitterness. The carbonation, although minimal, should be sufficient to cleanse the palate.

Bitter beer is traditionally a draught beer served from the barrel and owes much of its character to this means of dispensing. Draught beer must be primed with a little sugar to create conditioning gas and thus a slight measure of sparkle to the drink. Even from the cask, draught beer should never be entirely *flat*. And because they are drunk fairly quickly, bitter beers often possess a hint of residual sweetness due to these added priming sugars. BEST BITTER is a higher gravity, fuller bodied brew aimed at the person who enjoys good beer, but is satisfied by a pint or two of it. The increased malt content demands a higher hop rate to balance the natural sweetness it imparts over that of the primings. Original gravities range from 1035 to 1055 resulting in alcohol contents between 3.5 and 5.5 per cent by volume. In any brew, the degree of tolerable sweetness is proportional to the amount of carbonation. Meaning, from the drinker's point of view, a sweet gassy beer is not a thirst quencher. Thus bitter beer cannot be bottled as it stands. I can only think of two commercial bitter beers that are actually labelled as such.

Basically what happens is that the bitter beer is taken off after fermentation, is filtered, pasteurised, carbonated and then bottled without priming to give LIGHT ALE and PALE ALE from ordinary and best bitters respectively. Thus the bottled brews are gassier due to the artificial carbonation, drier in taste and appear to be more heavily hopped than the draught versions. Obviously brewers can, and do, make a special brew to produce one type if circumstances warrant it, but the basic sentiments on character should still hold true. I.P.A. or India Pale Ale originated from a special brew exported to the British Army in India before independence. To withstand the long journey it was necessary to increase the amount of hops used and keep the alcohol content high. Alcohol and hops are natural preservatives and the whole package results in a very palatable brew.

The ploy of producing a bottled and draught beer from one mash is also adopted for dark beers. MILD ALE is the quick consumption draught brew and BROWN ALE its bottled version. These are generally dark coloured, low alcohol, lightly hopped beers. A few light coloured mild ales exist and are quite valid brews simply devoid of the normal caramel or dark malt colouring agents.

The north of England has a good reputation for its dark beers and some kits are labelled NORTHERN MILD or BROWN ALE to capture this image. Scotland also boasts good regional ales characterised by a tangy malt flavour not found elsewhere. Thus you will come across kits aimed at producing this desirable flavour.

It seems to be the vogue these days to tag the word EXPORT to all sorts of beer. Presumably labelling the beer "export quality" instils the notion in the customer of a special high standard product endorsed by reputation and demand for sales abroad.

STOUT is a full bodied, dark textured brew. Produced using dark roasted grains and generous hops, the brew has excellent food value. Some are actually called NOURISHING STOUTS from this attribute. Mackeson and Guinness classify the two common styles in stouts and are found as SWEET STOUT and IRISH TYPE STOUT in kit form.

STRONG ALES and BARLEY WINES top the list for strength and some brews approach 10 per cent in alcohol content (as strong as table wine). Like wines they take a long time to ferment and the naturally conditioned ones, especially home brew versions, benefit enormously through maturation.

15

The rise in popularity of LAGER over the last few years has been quite phenomenal. Normally it is a very light coloured beer with a delicate hop flavour, crisp and refreshing to drink when served chilled. Much to some people's surprise, true lager is not a thin watery drink. CONTINENTAL LAGER is an all malt brew and has inherently more body than most English ales. And it is usually stronger as well. PILSNER is the low alcohol version for steady consumption. Dark versions of lager are rare as they are difficult to produce in the accepted image. To create an identity, and suggest authenticity, you will find more and more kits labelled MUNICH, BAVARIAN STYLE or other continental naming.

WE ARE BEING SERVED!

The home brew trade is now a mature industry with hundreds of retail outlets catering for all our needs in respect of equipment, ingredients and literature on the subject. Most retail outlets deal solely with the amateur wine and brewing trade, although there is an increasing trend for chemists, supermarkets and major shopping chains to devote a section or shelves to home brewing.

The range of products is quite incredible. It can be quite a daunting task for a beginner to stock up with all the necessary items. Explaining the basic process of brewing in terms of the equipment and ingredients required should instill sufficient confidence in the new home brewer to make a sensible and economical choice of products to suit his requirements.

CHAPTER 3

HOPPED WORTS

Hopped worts are the next logical step in home brewing for the beer kit brewer. Same quality and consistency, but more scope for practical flair.

In wanting to start brewing from "scratch" you will be looking for simple recipes which adequately demonstrate the process. By using HOPPED WORTS you learn the practical side quickly. Once the procedure has been grasped you can increase the choice of ingredients and embark on more exciting recipes using MALT EXTRACT.

Basic Brewing Process

Home brewed beer is mainly produced from malt extract syrup, hops, sugar, yeast and water and is a simple enough task to perform at home. Brewing is fundamentally cooking and was for centuries regarded as just another culinary skill. In those days the women folk did all the brewing and indeed it was deemed the wife's *duty* to brew the beer for the master of the household. Try imparting that gem of tradition to your spouse when handing her a Beer Kit for her birthday!

A quick glance at any of the recipes in this book will give an appreciation of the relative quantities and weights of the ingredients used for a batch of beer.

The first stage of the procedure is to boil up the malt extract, hops and sometimes roasted grain in water. After cooking the clear hopped wort is strained off into a fermenting bin and the liquid topped up with cold water. The "wort" (pronounced "wert"), as it is now called, is fermented into "beer" by the action of yeast. Yeast converts the sugar and the sugar in the malt extract into alcohol to give the beer strength. The beer is now rested for a while and finings added to assist clearing, before it is transferred again into bottles or a pressure barrel prior to drinking.

Getting Started

We want to start off and make a beer that is easy to brew. Fortunately it is possible to make the basic home brewing method described above simpler by using hopped wort, a more versatile form of beer kit.

Hopped Wort

Malt extract is a concentrate made from the malt sugar washed from mashed malted barley. The normal home brewing procedure then is to reconstitute to its original volume by dilution with water and then boil it with hops; a lengthy and sometimes inconvenient job. A true Hopped Wort is a concentrate made *after* boiling. By effectively bypassing the boiling stage for you, it saves considerable time and effort which explains why hopped wort forms the basis of so many beer kits. In fact, Muntona, Cordon Brew and the 2 lb. size of the Edme range of Bitter, Brown Ale, Lager and Barley Wine are sold as kits complete with yeast. As the recommended instructions with some require a small boiling period of five minutes, I regard them as bridging the gap between kits and malt extract brewing. My beginner's recipes are based on a Hopped Wort of your choice as a natural progression in brewing technique for someone wanting to be a bit more adventurous than allowed to be when making a kit.

The range of hopped worts I have tried are:

Cordon Brew Hopped Wort (18 and 36 pint sizes)
Best Bitter, Lager, Light Ale, Brown Ale, Stout, Export Pale Ale, Mild Ale, Barley Wine, Burton XXXX Bitter.

Edme Hopped Worts (2, 7, 14, 28, 56 lb. tins)
Bitter, Brown Ale, Lager and Barley Wine.

Muntona Hopped Wort (1.0 kg. (2.2 lb.) 1.5 kg. (3.3 lb.))
Bitter and Lager.

Equipment to Get You Started

Large Saucepan or Boiling Pan

Eventually a boiler or boiling pan with a capacity of at least 3 gallons (15 litre) will prove an essential piece of brewing equipment. For these beginners recipes a large saucepan should be adequate. I used the base part of a pressure cooker for my experiments.

Plastic Fermenting Bin

There are so many custom built plastic buckets designed for home brewing that it is not worth improvising with anything else. Choose one, or preferably two, with a 25 litre capacity and a snap on lid.

Syphon Tube

A 2 m. length of plastic tubing is used for siphoning the brewed beer into bottles or a barrel.

Beer Bottles

As a beginner, only use genuine beer bottles. These can either be saved after drinking the contents from commercial bottled beers or purchased new. A means of resealing them again is necessary,

Plastic press on reseal caps are cheap and easy to apply. The proper metal crown caps are the best, but one must invest in a capsuling tool as discussed later on page. A packet of beer labels will give the finishing touches to the brew.

Draught Beer Containers

Some styles of beers, particularly bitter and mild, taste better when served as draught beer. There is a range of suitable containers available, ranging from flexible polypins to the rigid plastic pressure barrels. The details given in Chapter 6 on these vessels should enable you to come to a decision as to the appropriate one for your requirements.

Beer Hydrometer and Jar

The Hydrometer is a small glass float which can indicate when a beer is *safe* to bottle. An inexperienced person can be misled by some brewing instructions and bottle beer prematurely and risk an explosion through the build up of excessive gas pressure. A simple measurement with the instrument highlights this danger.

Sterilising Chemicals

All brewing equipment must be maintained clean and sterile to avoid bacterial contamination and spoilage of the beer. A jar of sodium metabisulphite powder will cope with the hygiene side of brewing for many a batch of beer. To assist cleaning, a bottle brush would be a worthwhile investment now as well.

Miscellaneous Items

A small funnel, kitchen scales, spoons and saucepans will be required from time to time during the brewing process.

Beginners Recipes (Using Hopped Worts)

Each can of hopped wort will have brewing instructions and suggested recipes on it which obviously you can follow if you wish. For simplicity in demonstrating some practical aspects I will ask you to follow my common method of brewing for all the makes of hopped wort used in the recipes.

RECIPES TO TRY

2 GALLONS LAGER

Ingredients:

2 lb. tin Edme hopped lager wort
½ lb. white sugar
Yeast provided

2 GALLONS BITTER

Ingredients:

2 lb. tin Edme pale ale hopped wort
½ lb. brown sugar
Yeast provided

18 PINTS BROWN ALE

Ingredients:

Tin of Cordon Brew brown ale hopped wort
¾ lb. glucose chips
Yeast provided

18 PINTS STOUT

Ingredients:

Tin of Cordon Brew stout hopped wort
¾ lb. dark brown sugar
Yeast provided

5 GALLONS LAGER

Ingredients:

1.5 kg. tin Muntona lager hopped wort
1 kg. white sugar
Yeast provided

5 GALLONS BITTER

Ingredients:

1.5 kg. tin Muntona bitter hopped wort
1 kg. soft dark brown sugar
Yeast provided

Many more recipes based on hopped worts are included in the main recipe section for you to try.

Method:

Boiling up. Open the can of hopped extract and pour into the boiling pan. On cold days it pays to stand the tin in a bowl of hot water for a few minutes to make the syrup pour easier. The remaining extract sticking to the inside of the tin can be removed by rinsing out with two "tinfuls" of hot water. These washings must be added to the boiler. Stir the extract solution thoroughly so no smears of neat syrup adhere to the pan bottom. If you have sufficient boiler capacity (i.e. not more than three-quarters full) stir in the sugar quota as well. Apply heat to raise the mixture up to boiling point. Stir occasionally, keeping a watchful eye on progress as boiling point approaches. A thick scum will form, building up with amazing rapidity, and must be contained by stirring or reducing the applied heat. Simmer the wort for 5 minutes.

Into the fermenting bin. Meanwhile clean and sterilise the fermenting bin. Wash it out thoroughly then swill in a pint of hot water to which 1 teaspoon of sodium metabisulphite powder has been added. Wet all the inside surface and allow it to stand for a few minutes before pouring off. It is not necessary to rinse again.

Add 1 gallon (5 litres) of *cold* water before pouring in the boiled hopped wort. If the sugar could not be dealt with during the wort boil it can be added now. Dissolve it in some boiling water first.

Cold tap water can now be added to top up the brew to the desired 16, 18 or 40 pint level as appropriate.

Fermentation. When the brew has cooled to room temperature scatter the contents of the sachet of yeast on to the surface and place the lid of the bin on loosely.

Fermentation will normally take from three to ten days depending on the temperature. Keep the brew in a reasonably warm place. By reasonable, I mean between 16–19°C., the normal temperature indoors. Hot airing cupboards and cold garages should not be considered.

Remove any dirty substances brought up by the yeast. Stir and rouse the brew twice daily with a sterilised spoon to keep the yeast in suspension.

In the latter stages we look for signs that the fermentation is coming to an end. Normally, the yeast head disappears, leaving a thin ring of foam over the surface. Beneath, the brew can be seen to be visibly clearing and bubble activity is slight. However, this visual check must be backed up by simply tasting the beer to see that it is no longer sweet. If it is, the fermentation must be prolonged. Manufacturers of hopped worts and kits usually quote specific gravity readings as a guide for assessing the end of fermentation. Hydrometer readings below 1005 are normally regarded as signs that the beer can be bottled safely.

Settling.

Certain malt concentrates contain clearing agents to ensure the beer falls bright enough in the bin to be bottled immediately the fermentation has finished. If yours does, then go ahead and bottle. However, the beer is at a vulnerable stage whilst awaiting for the yeast to fall out and clear and I would advise transferring it to another vessel or vessels where settling can take place under sterile conditions. One gallon glass demi-john jars fitted with airlocks are ideal for this purpose.

If you do not possess the extra containers simply add two crushed Campden tablets to the beer and snap on the fermenting bin lid tightly. Leave for two days undisturbed before proceeding with bottling.

Racking.

Siphoning, or racking as we call it in home brewing, is the gentlest means of transferring the beer to another container with the minimum of disturbance to the yeast deposit in the bin. Any scum or yeast on the surface of the brew must be skimmed off before starting. Syphon off all the beer except for the sediment. Each recipient container must be filled to just below the airlock bung, leaving a 2 cm. space. Insert the airlocks and bungs. Storing the racked beer in a slightly cooler environment than that for the initial ferment will assist clarification. All well made beer will clear naturally. Artificial clearing aids are often employed but they are not necessary with these recipes. A few days stand will allow the beer to clear adequately. Starbright beer is definitely not wanted at this stage because a minute amount of yeast must be carried over to condition the beer later on.

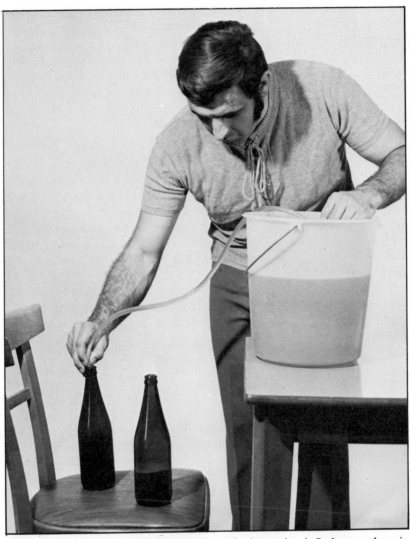

Siphoning: Gravity forces liquid to settle at the lowest level. So long as there is continuity of liquid (as in a full tube) between containers at different levels, a flow will maintained. Liquid will even flow up out of the top bin appearing to defy gravity before it falls into the lower jar.

The rate of flow is governed by the difference in levels (head of liquid) and the bore of the tube. Siphoning can be stopped by raising the outlet end above the liquid level in the upper bin. These simple manoeuvres give control of fluid transfer.

Maturation. Most of these beginners beers should be drinkable four or five days after bottling. They will not be at their best as this only comes with adequate maturation. Even so, I reckon they peak with condition, clarity and flavour in about three weeks, and are best drunk within two months of bottling.

In a barrel. All the above recipes can be put in a plastic barrel for dispensing on draught if required. Basically all bulk containers must be primed using the same rate as for bottled beers (e.g. 2 oz. per 5 gallons). There are so many different barrels, casks and polypins, that it would be worthwhile reading ahead to Chapter 6 to check the recommended procedure for your particular one.

Bottling. Collect sufficient bottles for the job. Inspect them for chips and cracks and reject any suspect ones. Make sure you possess sufficient stoppers for the bottles. Thoroughly cleanse the bottles, using no more than a bottle brush and hot water. Afterwards rinse out each bottle; first with stock sterilising solution and finally with cold water.

To generate more CO_2 gas to condition the flat beer, the fermentation must be rekindled by adding a small amount of sugar to each bottle. Experience has shown that a $\frac{1}{2}$ teaspoon per pint (5 ml. per litre) is just the right amount. This priming sugar, as we call it, can be funnelled into the neck of each bottle. Different sized bottles must be primed on a pro rata basis.

Filling. Syphon the beer into the bottles. Keep the end of the syphon tube near the bottom of the bottles to avoid frothing. It is essential that the bottles are not completely filled. Leave an airspace; a minimum of $\frac{3}{4}$ inch per pint or 40 mm. per litre bottle. Fit the appropriate bottle seals and labels if required.

Store the bottled beer in a warm place for a few days to allow secondary conditioning to take place and then transfer to a cooler environment to restore clarity and assist maturation.

EASY MADE MALT EX

1. COLLECT THE INGREDIENTS...

For 5 gallons/25 litres, you will need:-
4 lb Malt Extract (2 kg).
½ lb Crystal Malt Grains (250 gm).
1 lb Brown Sugar (500 gm).
3 oz Hops (preferably Goldings)(100 gm).
1 sachet Dried Yeast.

...AND PREPARE THEM

Weigh out ingredients.
Open and stand can of
malt extract in hot water.
Crush the malt grains.
Activate yeast by mixing
with a little cold sugar water.

2. BOILING

Dissolve the malt extract and sugar in
2 to 3 gallons of hot water in the
boiler before switching on the heat.
Add the hops, apply heat and boil
for 45 minutes.
Add the crushed crystal malt for the
last 5 minutes.

3. COLLECT THE HOPPED WORT

Clean and sterilise the intended
fermentation bin.
Strain off the liquid through a
sieve to separate the redundant
solids.
Top up to the 5 gallon mark
with cold water.

RACT BITTER BEER

4. FERMENTATION

Cool to room temperature.
Pitch in yeast and loosely cover
with lid.
Ferment for 4 to 8 days depending
on temperature (ideal 18°C.).
Stir brew daily and remove any dirty scum.

5. SETTLING AND CLARIFICATION

When fermentation is almost complete
(hydrometer reading below 1005) add 2
crushed campden tablets and requisite
dose of beer finings.
Snap fermentation bin lid on tightly and
leave for 3 days for beer to clear.

6. SIPHON OFF, EITHER...

...INTO BOTTLES

Clean and sterilise bottles.
Prime each pint bottle with ½
teaspoonful of sugar (5gm/ltr).
Fill bottle using siphon and
leave ¾" air space (40 ml/ltr).
Fit closures to bottles.

OR INTO PRESSURE BARREL

Clean and sterilise barrel.
Add 2oz sugar (60gm) and
siphon in beer.
Fit gas injector unit or plain
filler cap as required.

7. READY FOR DRINKING

Keep beer in warm place for 1 week,
then transfer to a cooler environment
for another week or so to mature.
Then start supping your efforts.
But take it steady.
Easy made bitter is
much stronger than
most pub beers.

SERVING YOUR BEER

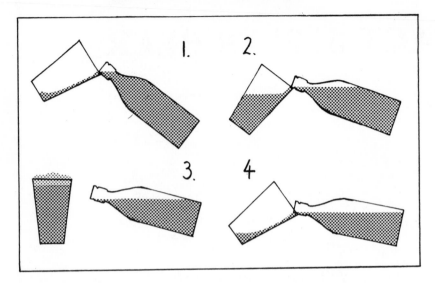

HOME BREWED BEER generally contains a small amount of yeast deposited as a sediment over the bottom of the bottle. The yeast will tend to lift and cloud the beer when the bottle is opened.

To minimise this disturbance and maintain clarity, pour the beer into the glass with one continuous tilting motion, pausing only if two glasses require filling. Stop filling when the sediment rises to the bottle neck.

CHAPTER 4

INGREDIENTS
FOR MALT EXTRACT BREWING

Malt extract syrups laid the foundation for modern home brewing to become the country's favourite leisure pastime. The satisfying reward of drinking first class beers brewed at a fraction of bar prices attracts thousands of new devotees to the hobby each year.

Guided by experienced techniques perfected by years of practice (and drinking!) by the author, you can choose a recipe or select the right malt, hops, roast grain, sugar and yeast to create some really superb brews yourself.

Let us now take a closer look at these ingredients and the equipment we will need.

MALT EXTRACT

Malt extract in its various guises forms the basis for all the beers in this book and is the most expensive single ingredient. It can be purchased in a liquid form as a thick viscous brown syrup or as a dry powder. Even these forms can be subdivided for different types and colours of extract. Some of the most popular or useful brands are discussed.

Boots (2, 4 lb. tins)

A straightforward economical extract employing burnt sugar (caramel) to impart a nice golden brown tint to the finished beer. Thus this one is best suited to brewing English style beers.

Edme D.M.S. (2, 7, 14, 28, 56 lb. tins)

Edme D.M.S. was the forerunner of all malt extracts for the home brew trade. D.M.S. means Diastatic Malt Extract; the term diastatic refers to its ability to convert other cereal starch to brewing sugar. This characteristic offers tremendous variety and scope with brewing recipes and is used extensively for "mashed" beers in Chapter 8. The 2 lb. and 14 lb. tins seem to be the most popular choice of home brew customers.

Edme S.F.X. (2, 7, 14, 28, 56 lb. tins)

Super Flavex is a standard non-diastatic syrup with added caramel. The additional colouring makes this syrup ideal for brewing dark beers. Actually it is not too dark for bitter or pale ale production, and I find it in many instances to be more versatile than D.M.S.

The larger cans of D.M.S. and S.F.X. are really worth considering on economic grounds. Any extract left in an opened tin will remain sound for months so long as it is sealed down again immediately after use. Occasionally the extract may crystallise in storage as honey is prone to do, but this temporary change of state does not affect the brewing quality at all.

Itona C.A.

Specifically designed with a Controlled Analysis to ensure the home brewer has just the right balance of fermentable sugars. 2 lb. tins.

Muntona

A full range of liquid extracts are listed. National, a lager malt extract,comes in 1 kg. tins, whereas the light, medium and dark are supplied in 1½ kg. tins. Century has probably the highest diastatic activity extract for home brewing, but as with the standard Malamalt, it can only be purchased in 25 kilo drums.

Paines

Paines supply the malt extract and hopped worts for many kits. Their range of light, amber and dark liquid extracts are now available in 1 kg. and 12½ kg. tins.

Light Dried Malt Extract (1, 2, 7 lb. packs)

Malt extract syrups contain about 20 per cent water. Light dried malt extract is standard syrup with the water removed. Consequently it is all malt goodness and proportionately more expensive. As a powder it is easier to handle than the syrup variety so long as it is kept moisture free. Particular attention must be paid to keeping it dry when only a portion of the pack is used.

Dark Dried Malt Extract (1, 2, 7 lb. packs)

This is the caramelised version of the light dried and is used in dark brews as is the liquid variety.

HOPS

Hops are an essential brewing ingredient used to flavour and bitter the beer. The traditional brewing practice calls for the whole hop cones to be boiled with the malt extract to leach out the bittering and preservative substances. The boiling process is still, and must be, practised today, but not necessarily with *whole* hops. Whole hops are notoriously difficult to keep fresh and the problem is aggravated when bulk supplies are packaged into small sizes for home brew shops. Thus the home brew industry is taking a leaf out of the commercial boys' book and rapidly changing over to processed hops.

Pelleted Hops

Pelleted hops are simply shredded whole hops which have been reconstituted into granules without the redundant petal fibres. All the lupulin goodness and bittering substances are retained. Since the process is purely mechanical the flavour is unaltered and freshness is assured during manufacture by sealing the hop pellets in nitrogen sealed bags. Excluding oxygen prevents the deterioration suffered by whole hops stored in adverse conditions. However, pelleted hops can suffer the same fate if they are not sold in nitrogen sealed or airtight containers.

Whole hops suit the home brewing process better than pellets from a practical standpoint, but on balance I reckon the superior flavour, easier storage and better shelf life of processed hops outweighs the slight inconvenience in their use.

Hops are best stored at home in the deep freezer or refrigerator. Failing these ideals, any cool dark dry place will suit.

COMPARISON OF HOP VARIETIES

VARIETY	Relative Bitterness (% Alpha Acid)	ORIGIN, CHARACTER AND USE
Goldings	5.0	Fine English hop. Bitter, Pale, Light
Fuggles	4.5	Good all round hop. All types
Northern Brewer	7.0	Fairly strong hop. Dark beers
Bullion	8.5	Very strong flavour and aroma. Dark beers
Bramling Cross	5.5	Good flavour hops for light brews
W.G.V.	5.0	As Bramlings
Northdown	8.0	Fuggles substitute
Challenger	7.0	Goldings substitute
Target	9.5	Very strong, use with caution } New Varieties
Saxon	7.0	Good flavour and aroma
Viking	7.0	Good flavour and aroma
Hallertau	8.0	Hard to beat for flavour—German hop
Saaz	7.0	Probably finest Lager hop—Czech origin
Styrian Goldings	7.0	Nice bitter Lager hop, English Light brews
Cluster	7.5	American hops—Popular hop, reasonable flavour
Talisman	8.0	American hops—Better than Cluster
Pride of Ringwood	9.0	American hops—Coarse hop
Brewers Gold	10.0	American hops—Relative of Bullion, very strong
Cascade	6.0	American hops—Best American hop for flavour

The advent of pelleted hops has meant that most retailers can afford to stock a larger range of named hop varieties. There are about a dozen types used in my recipes.

Constituents of Hops

Hops, in common with all fruits and flowers, are found as numerous varieties each with its own character. The active brewing constituents contributing to the flavour, bittering power and aroma are found in the resins, essential oils and the tannins of the dried hop cones. Mainly it is the Humulon soft resin which contributes to hop bitterness and antiseptic properties. Measurement of the resin, referred to as Alpha Acid, is used for valuation and comparison of hop bitterness between varieties.

The traditional hops, such as Goldings and Fuggles, are gradually being replaced by stronger varieties both in bittering power and disease resistance. Strength brings coarseness and the majority of the new economy hops cannot match the fine flavours of their predecessors. Seedless hops, once used exclusively for lagers, are reckoned to possess a better flavour than seeded ones and research is still going on to find strains suitable of standing up to the vagrancies of the wet climate in Britain.

The essential oils are largely responsible for the aroma of the hop. Much of the fragrance is lost when the hops are boiled in the malt wort and techniques such as staggered dosing and dry hopping must be resorted to, to offset this loss.

In brewing coppers where only whole hops are used, the physical size and shape of the cones and petals creates a buffering effect in the boiling wort and accelerates the clearing of the malt from dissolved protein. Tannin in the strigs and petals assists the coagulation of protein matter as well. Pelleted or powdered hops obviously cannot do the job so well and allowances must be made.

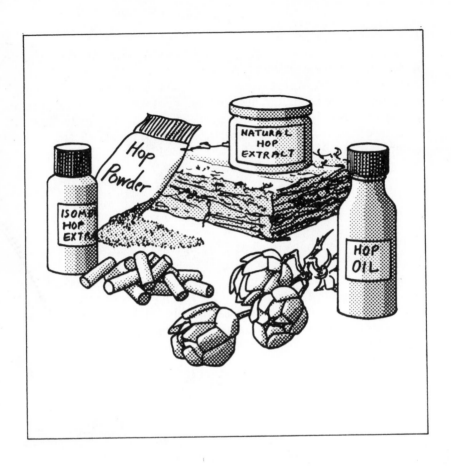

Here are some of the forms in which hops are available to the home brewer, as discussed in this chapter – from left to right, isomerised hop extract, hop powder, hop pellets, hop extract, compressed dried hops, fresh hops and hop oil. All have their uses, advantages and, sometimes, disadvantages, as explained.

HOP PRODUCTS

1. *Fresh Hops.* Dried whole cones of female flower of the Hop Bine. The traditional form of this ingredient. Bitterness and flavour extracted by boiling with malt.

2. *Compressed Hops.* Fresh hops compressed into a slab have better keeping qualities.

3. *Pellet Hops.* Mechanically shredded and reconstituted hop cones. The modern form of hops. Two types are available:
   a. Non concentrated type; 4 parts equivalent to 5 parts whole hops.
   b. Hopfix type; 1 part equivalent to 2 parts whole hops. Requires boiling as per whole hops.

4. *Powdered Hops.* Powdered hop pellets sold in nitrogen sealed sachets. Use as recommended.

5. *Hop Extract.* A concentrated syrup of hop goodness. Must be boiled like whole hops to extract bitterness.

6. *Isomerised Hop Extract.* Does not require boiling and can be used after fermentation to increase bitterness.

7. *Essential Oil of Hops.* Aroma extract used to restore hop bouquet.

HOP EXTRACTS

The active brewing resins and oils can be extracted as a thick viscous syrup. Normally referred to as HOP EXTRACT or HOP NATURA, the concentrated syrup must be apportioned carefully and *boiled* with the wort just like whole hops. The flavour can be very good indeed and these extracts can maintain their freshness for a very long period if resealed immediately after use.

The natural humulon resin in the hop cone is not very bitter in itself until it has been *isomerised* in the wort boil, a lengthy process taking about one hour to achieve. ISOMERISED HOP EXTRACT (Iso Hoppon) is a concentrate made after this chemical change has taken place. Thus this type of extract can be added to increase the bitterness of the final beer. The potential is enormous when using the right type of malt extract as the tedious and often inconvenient boiling process of home brewing can be bypassed. However, it is only fair to say that these extracts are generally inferior regards flavour to normal hop extracts and fresh hops. There are a number of named varieties available giving a wide and versatile choice of hops for your brewing.

HOP OIL or ESSENTIAL OIL OF HOPS is an *aroma* extract completely devoid of bitterness. Just a few drops prior to bottling or casking effectively "dry hops" the brew and restores the fresh hop aroma often lost in the wort boil.

Compressed Hops

Fresh hops have better keeping qualities when compressed into slabs. The rectangular block of solid hop cones is easily divided and cut with a knife to give an accurate amount without weighing.

ROASTED MALT GRAINS

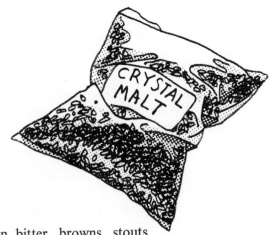

The difference between bitter, browns, stouts and lager is largely due to the integration and selections of roast grain in the recipe. In our case, the flavour and colour is extracted from the crushed malt simply by boiling it in the wort.

Crystal Malt

Crystal malt is the perfect partner for malt extract syrup providing smoothness and body often lacking in these concentrates. The malt is roasted in the wet state after the germination stage of processing so that the grain kernels are converted to a type of crystalline sugar, slightly caramelised. In some countries, crystal malt is actually referred to as CARAMEL MALT. A useful additive for all beer styles.

Black Malt or Patent Black Malt

A high roasted malt burnt almost to carbonisation. The intense colour and rich luscious taste is much sought after in dark brews. It is by far the best roasted malt for colouring beer from slight tinting in dark lagers to the deep reddish-garnet hues of full bodied stouts.

Normally, in commercial brewing, the dark goodness is extracted from the grain during the mashing process. Boiling is a harsh treatment and special care must be taken to avoid leaching out unwanted flavours. This reasoning applies to all dark malts. My recipes cater for this condition by recommending lower grain quotas than for mashed beers, using the correct water treatment and suggesting limited boiling times.

Chocolate Malt

Chocolate Malt is really "underdone" Patent Black Malt. Consequently it is lighter in colouring and flavouring power. The texture is completely different and not just simply a dilute version of black. Consequently you cannot reduce the quota of black malt in a brew to achieve the character of chocolate. It is unsurpassed in the production of sweet stouts. High malt contents impart a tremendous depth of flavour, smooth, without being overpowering. Regards colouring, it is a poor agent. The plain chocolate colour of the grain is the right shade for a thick stout. However, when diluted for mild or brown ale production, it appears as a dirty brown hue and must be disguised; usually by adding caramel colouring.

Roast Barley

The economic way to darken a brew and retain malt flavour is to employ roasted barley. By roasting the raw barley before going to the trouble of malting it, should in theory make it cheaper, but this is not often so in home brewing.

Malting means mellowness and thus roast barley is inherently coarser than roast malts. The iron-like flavour is accountable by the relatively high acid content. Carbonate, chalky and consequently alkaline waters present the ideal brewing balance for roasted barley and lends itself to the production of dry Irish type stouts. Guinness is the prime example of the success of this blend.

Crushing Malts

The crushing of roasted grains is not so critical as for the pale, lager and other extract bearing malts. Coffee mills, blenders or even improvising with a rolling pin to crush the grain will prove satis-

Home-made malt mill

factory. Somewhere between the whole grain and a fine powder should be your aim. The electric devices are rarely capable of producing an even crush of particle size and hence you must compromise. Most of the grains mentioned can be purchased already crushed for your convenience.

MANY OTHER GRAINS AND CEREALS SOLD AS BREWING INGREDIENTS ARE ONLY RELEVANT TO MASHING RECIPES AND ARE DISCUSSED LATER IN CHAPTER 8.

SUGAR AND SYRUPS

It is sound practice to include a measure of sugar in nearly all malt extract beer recipes. Besides being the cheapest source of fermentable extract, sugar helps to control the quality and flavour balance of the brew, gives alcoholic strength and speeds fermentation and subsequent maturation.

White Household Sugar

Granulated white sugar is pure sucrose and is entirely fermentable. It is produced from refined sugar cane or sugar beet and it is found in many forms. Cube, icing and caster sugars are all pure sucrose but are generally more expensive than the plain granulated form. Commercial breweries formulate their recipes around their cheapest source of sugar, which to them, is usually invert or maize syrups. White household sugar is our cheapest, and hence many recipes will call for its use.

Dark Household Sugars

Another reason why commercial breweries do not favour the inclusion of white sugar is because it is really too pure and devoid of residual flavour. Dark sugars, such as demerara, soft light brown, soft dark brown, Muscavado and Barbados impart a luscious tang to the brew. And so, in trying to capture the rich character of some good pub beers we must invest in their use as well.

Invert Sugar

Invert sugar (sometimes labelled CORN SUGAR or DEXTROSE) can be regarded as the standard brewing sugar. Ready made invert comes in the form of a crystalline mass containing approximately 10 per cent water. I have noticed that some blocks are blends containing up to half their weight as plain sucrose: a point to watch when assessing the economics of sugar values. Theoretically, invert must be preferred for brewing. This is because white sugar must first be "inverted" by the enzyme invertase in yeast before fermentation can commence, but in practice, I have not detected any time lag that could positively be attributed to this cause.

Brewing Sugar

Brewing sugar is a syrup of PURE INVERT SUGAR containing about 20 per cent water. Sometimes the syrup is laced with caramel colouring to suit a particular brewery's needs. Unfortunately, it is still relatively expensive in the home brew trade which is a pity because I would prefer to use more of it in my brews. Its taste and looks are like a delicate golden syrup.

Golden Syrup

Golden syrup is a partially inverted refiners syrup and thus has many desirable qualities for brewing. Tasted neat it may seem too strong in flavour and aroma, but carefully blended in a full brew it confers the character of proper brewing sugars. OLD FASHIONED CANE SYRUP is similar and is ideal for priming draught beers.

40

Glucose Chips

Glucose Chips are manufactured by the acid conversion of purified maize starch. The large chips of crystalline sugars contain about 10 per cent water and tend to ferment out drier than either cane or invert sugars. GLUCOSE POWDER is a purer version and imparts a rather fruity flavour to the beer.

Caramel

Sold as BREWERS CARAMEL or BEER COLOURING it does what the latter suggests. Basically it is just a concentrated solution of burnt sugar and will be used in recipes from the darkest stout to even the most delicate of lagers. Caramel tends to be a neglected ingredient in home brewing. Presumably the interest wanes once the flavour aspects have been mastered, but really a good looking and enticing brew should be our goal as well.

Treacles

Black treacle and molasses possess very strong pungent flavours. Again, with judicious dosing these thick viscous solutions of partially refined sugars are employable in stouts, winter ales and special brews.

Lactose

A certain degree of sweetness is desirable in most beers to balance the bitterness of the hops. In naturally conditioned home brewed beer where live yeast is in the bottle and acts on any sugar present, achieving the requisite degree of sweetness can be difficult. Lactose, a sweet tasting milk derivative, can not be fermented by normal brewery yeast and hence can be employed to overcome this problem. The white lactose powder has slight disadvantages in so much that its flavour can deteriorate quickly and its solubility in beer leaves much to be desired.

Barley Syrup

Malt extract is manufactured, as we know, from *malted* barley grains. Barley syrup on the other hand is made from *raw* barley chemically dosed to change its natural starch store into fermentable extract. In theory, bypassing the malting and mashing processes should make it cheaper than malt extract, but on the home brew shelves it is priced at about the same. If more home brew enthusiasts appreciated the virtues of barley syrup and created the demand the price could come down.

The flavour it imparts in beer is not so strong as malt based syrups. As the latter tends to possess a characteristic tang of over maltiness, barley syrup can act as a flavour dilutant, but at the same time maintaining the body and other quality balancing attributes of barley. When used in commercial breweries as an adjunct, it is often preferred to malt extract.

Artificial Sweeteners

Certain malt extract syrups ferment out too dry in flavour compared with mashed worts. Artificial sweeteners such as SACCHARIN can round off the flavour of such brews quite nicely without undue sweetness. More sweeteners can obviously be used where a sweet taste is required. SWEETEX LIQUID or WINE SWEETENER is easier for administering the dose. Approximately four drops give the equivalent sweetness of one level teaspoonful of sugar.

Malto Dextrin (Glucose Polymer)

Under trade names of BURTON BODY BREW or DEXTRINE these products contain a high percentage of unfermentable sugars that give extra body to the brew. Some malt extracts are deficient in dextrin content and these products help to restore the correct balance and improve overall flavour.

WATER

It is a sobering thought that even our strongest brews are nearly all water! An important ingredient as all domestic water supplies contain minute quantities of mineral salts that can have a marked influence on the brewing process and the subsequent quality of the finished beer. Water treatment is often needed to brew a range of beer styles successfully.

Early brewers found, presumably by trial and error, some areas to be more suited for brewing one type of beer than others. The fame of the Burton area for pale ale production, Dublin for stouts and the

London area for dark sweetish brews is well known. It was only when scientific knowledge advanced to an understanding of the chemical reactions of brewery processes that the effects of dissolved mineral salts in the water supply were fully appreciated. From then it was a relatively easy step to devise water treatments to enable breweries to produce any beer style.

In home brewing water treatment has been a much misunderstood topic. Its mystery has attracted the blame for more beer disorders than any other cause.

The main reason for water treatment is simply for acid adjustment and is dependent on the ingredients used and the method employed. Starting brewing by mashing the barley malt as in commercial practice, water treatment must rate serious attention. With malt extract brews much of the emphasis is lost. The manufacturer of the malt syrup has already done the hard work and we only need to consider the boiling process. Taking it a stage further to making beer kits where no process chemical changes occur, water treatment is not required at all

For simple basic malt extract brewing there are plenty of proprietary water treatments available or you can formulate your own from the various mineral salts.

So let's see what is needed. The first step is to decide what type of water supply you are fed with. Broadly, domestic water supplies can be categorised into three groups and are easily identified by the layman. A quick telephone call to your local Water Authority would solve any doubts on the matter.

Permanently Hard

Waters termed permanently hard have high concentrations of calcium and magnesium sulphates which are essential for pale ale, bitter and light ale productions.

Soft Water

Very low salt content that really does feel soft to the touch. When lathered with soap or detergents it produces copious supplies of foam. An ideal brewing water for lagers and one which readily accepts treatment for other brews.

Temporary Hard

Certain hard waters can be rendered soft by boiling. Sulphates are not affected by boiling and thus are termed permanently hard. However, on boiling chalky water, the hard salt calcium bicarbonate becomes unstable and precipitates out of solution as the insoluble calcium carbonate salt. Temporary hard waters are inherently alkaline. Thus used straight from the tap, these waters can subtly tone down high acid ingredients such as roast barley. Alternatively, the water can be boiled first and the soft water drawn off the cooled precipitate. The softer water can then be treated as appropriate.

Rainwater

Remember that it is easier to add salts to water than to remove unwanted ones from it. I live in a very chalky area and for some sophisticated brews using mashing I find the high level of chalk inconvenient. Often I have not got the time to boil all my brewing water to reduce the chalk level, hence I resort to using rainwater. Clear rainwater, or even melted snow, by itself is excellent for producing lager. Its most useful role, however, is in diluting the salt content of other water sources. Be sensible about collecting rainwater and ensure it does not pass a toxic path. I safeguard against impurity by passing the rainwater through a wine filter and then dose in a requisite amount of sodium metabisulphite sterilising powder ($\frac{1}{2}$ teaspoon per 5 gallons). Alternatively, the water can be passed through a MAYREI Water Filter. The unit also plugs on to the tap to remove chlorine level and other impurities from your domestic supply.

Water Treatment

Water treatment can be a very complex subject dependent on so many variables that further discussion of the intricacies would more likely confuse than help the reader at this stage in brewing where we are only concerned with basic malt extract recipes. The finer points are discussed when appropriate throughout the text and is especially relevant during the subject of mashing in Chapter 8.

The treatments recommended below should be carried out on the water used for boiling the wort and unless stated in proprietary pack instructions, the dosage is for 5 gallons (25 litres) and should be apportioned pro rata.

WATER TREATMENT FOR 5 GALLONS OF BREWING WATER

Your water supply is:	Soft	Permanently Hard	Temporarily Hard (Chalky)
The beer needs:			
Bitter, Pale Ale, Light Ale	A	None	A, C
Brown Ale, Mild Ale, Sweet Stout	B	B	None
Dry Stout	D	D	None
Lager	None	E	C, E

A. *Pale Ale/Bitter Water Treatment.* Use proprietary packs as recommended on instructions, or make your own from:
  4 parts gypsum (calcium sulphate)
  1 part common salt (sodium chloride)
  1 part Epsom salts (magnesium sulphate)
Using 2 level teaspoons of the mixture per 5 gallons (10 ml./25 litres).

B. *Mild Ale/Brown Ale Water Treatment.* Use proprietary packs as recommended on instructions, or make your own from:
  1 part Epsom salts (magnesium sulphate)
  1 part common salt (sodium chloride)
Use 1 level teaspoon per 5 gallons (5 ml./25 litres)

C. *Lactic Acid Water Treatment.* Lactic acid is the safest acid to use for beer water treatment. It comes in liquid form. Use 1 teaspoon per 5 gallons. In lieu, citric acid can be used, but is not really recommended, but it is better than using nothing at all.

D. *Precipitate of Chalk* (*Calcium Carbonate*). Use 1 level teaspoon per 5 gallons

E. *Rainwater* (*or Distilled*). If practicable, use 4 parts rainwater to 1 from the tap. Ensure it comes from a safe source and is sterilised before use. Failure to dilute your unsympathetic water supply will just make your lager taste a bit like a light ale. The choice is yours!

DRIED YEAST

Select a general purpose brewing yeast. Edme, Boots, Cordon Brew, Vina, Vierka and Unican varieties are particularly good as they are sufficiently viable to be pitched in the beer without having to make up a yeast starter bottle first.

Individual sachets marked "sufficient for 5 gallons" are ideal, although I prefer to err on the safe side and use two per brew. Some yeasts are sold in tubs. These are certainly cheaper, but do not buy too large a size. Select a size which can be confidently used up in two months of brewing.

Dried yeast will get you under way with brewing, but later on you may consider using commercial brewery yeasts or genuine yeast cultures to give that extra edge of quality to your beers.

CHAPTER 5

BREWING ACTIVITIES

The Beer Kit, Hopped Wort and Easy Malt Extract recipes outline the fundamental sequences of boiling, fermentation, bottling and casking of home brewed beers. Your brewing has got to fit into the household routine and available free time. The method must be flexible enough to suit the brewing equipment at hand and whatever limitations that may impose.

Writing instructions loose enough to cover all the types of brewing equipment and personal restrictions is totally inadequate. Embarking on one detailed method throws up all sorts of queries and further guidance is often required for the specialised pieces of gear. I know only too well that home brewers will adapt, modify, short circuit and leave out stages if the brewing method proves inconvenient. Brewing ideals are rarely commensurate with practical convenience and I acknowledge this in my approach.

The options are listed, together with the advantages and disadvantages, so that you can decide on matters such as yeast selection, length of boil, methods of secondary care and maturation in the bottle or cask. Some of the latest equipment on the market is introduced, with guidance and advice on the operating procedures and in-service conditions.

All in all, I want to instill sufficient confidence in you to look at my recipes, check on how they fit with your brewing circumstances and be bold enough to make changes as and if necessary. And to have the brewing acumen to judge accurately what these changes will bring.

CLEANING AND STERILISING

Conducting your brewing under clean and sterile conditions is essential. More home brewed beer is ruined by inattention to production hygiene than from any other cause. We can only prevent infection, not cure it.

Having a bad tummy after drinking home brewed beer should never happen, but it does. A beer can become infected without tasting so and can catch the drinker unawares: a most embarrassing situation for the host and an uncomfortable experience for the recipient. Prevention is easy, but attention to the hygiene side at all stages of brewing is essential.

All foodstuffs prepared in the home are susceptible to bacterial contamination and will eventually go off if not stored under the right conditions. Brewing beer is a relatively long domestic process conducted at temperatures where spoilage organisms thrive. Consequently the normal standards of kitchen hygiene can be inadequate and it is advisable to rely on the readily available chemical sterilisers. There are plain sterilisers and combined detergent sterilisers, each with very definite duties. The home brewer must understand their usage as some can be used in the beer, whereas others would poison it. Washing-up liquids are not recommended for cleaning brewing equipment as traces of detergents can affect the foam head of the beer.

Choosing the Right Equipment

Modern day plastics and glassware are easy to keep clean and are used extensively for home brew equipment. Nearly all cases of brew infections arise from deposits of yeast and dregs left on the equipment. Scrupulously washing or scrubbing each item visibly clean after use will eliminate much of this risk. Only use cleaning aids which will not scratch the surface of plastic products. Hot water and a nylon scouring pad will deal with the task of cleaning the larger more accessible items.

Bottle cleaning is a long and tedious job and my improvisations shown on page 49 will save a great deal of effort. Special bottle brushes can be purchased for this job.

The chamois leather scourer is the invention of Mr David Stacey, of Letchworth, Herts.

Sterilising Agents

The two types of sterilising agents commonly used in home brewing are based on sulphur dioxide or chlorine.

Chlorine is by far the best sterilising agent, but unfortunately in large doses it can be dangerous if not handled sensibly. Sulphur dioxide is less toxic under normal conditions.

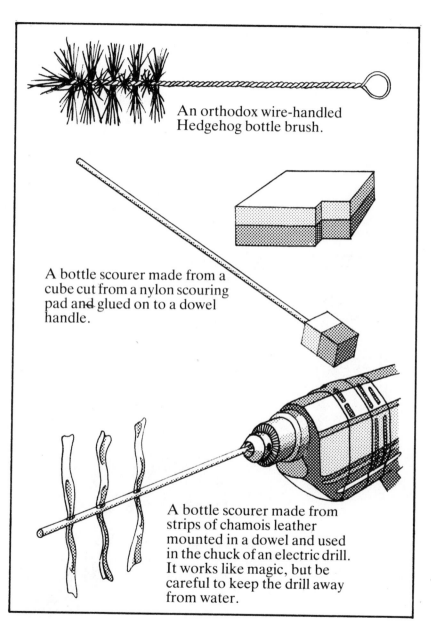

An orthodox wire-handled Hedgehog bottle brush.

A bottle scourer made from a cube cut from a nylon scouring pad and glued on to a dowel handle.

A bottle scourer made from strips of chamois leather mounted in a dowel and used in the chuck of an electric drill. It works like magic, but be careful to keep the drill away from water.

Some useful bottle cleaners.

Sodium Metabisulphite

Commonly abbreviated to "Sodium Met" by home brewers, the chemical is a convenient source of sulphur dioxide and is still the most versatile sterilising agent available to us. By varying the strength of the solution, it can be used for sterilising equipment and can be added to the beer as a preservative.

Sterilising Solution

Dissolve 1 teaspoon of powder in 1 pint of water or 10 ml. in 1 litre.

To sterilise a piece of equipment, simply wash all the surface area with the solution and allow it to stand for a few minutes. Drain well. Normally there is no need to rinse, and indeed, rinsing with tap water could lead to problems with some domestic water supplies. The solution should be discarded afterwards.

Handy Dispenser

An empty washing-up liquid container cleansed of its original contents makes an ideal dispenser for small quantities of stock solution. The solution is effective so long as a pungent smell of gas can be detected.

A few drops to keep an empty bottle sweet during storage.

Campden Tablets

Two tablets crushed and dissolved in 1 pint of water makes the normal sterilising strength solution. One tablet in a gallon of beer is maximum preservative level allowed in commercial brews.

> **THE FOLLOWING CHLORINE BASED STERI-LISERS MUST NOT COME INTO CONTACT WITH THE BEER AT ANY STAGE OF ITS PRODUCTION.**

Chempro S.D.F.

A quick acting combination cleanser/steriliser used by commercial breweries and now readily available to the home brew trade. The white powder is made up to varying strengths depending on the task. Comprehensive instructions are given on the packet.

V.W.P.

This powder steriliser/cleanser/deodoriser, made up in hot or tepid water, is ideal for cleaning heavily contaminated vessels and containers.

Antimycin

Effective against all bacteria and fungi, including wild yeasts and spoilage organisms. The contact time required is only a few minutes. Antimycin is very economical. Even when made up as the normal dilute solution it has an indefinite shelf life regarding its sterilising properties. I have a large dustbin filled with antimycin solution for batch sterilising of bottles.

Antimycin-Detergent-Steriliser

Similar to the straight steriliser, but has blended with it a special detergent which will facilitate the washing of all apparatus, vessels and bottles, and at the same time sterilise them.

PPH Descaler-Detergent

A most effective way of removing all forms of organic deposit (yeast films, moulds etc.) from brewing containers. As this solution can be used repeatedly it is a useful alternative to the antimycin.

B.H.C. Steriliser-Detergent

Another economical steriliser detergent capable of being effective despite constant usage.

Household Bleach

The plain, not with detergents or pine extracts, is a very effective and economical steriliser and cleanser. Just half an eggcup in one gallon will ensure complete sterility and doubling up the strength helps to remove stubborn deposits as well.

BOILING

Opposition to the smell and clouds of billowing steam can make lengthy boiling sessions indoors impractical. Complete boils are easier outside with the right equipment, but by observing a few facts about the malt syrup and the hops, the process can be conducted inside quite satisfactorily.

The traditional brewing method is followed by the "all grain mash technique" used by some home brewers. Here a dilute solution of sweet malt sugar, approximately equal to the final volume of the beer to be brewed, is washed out of the mashed grains. Hops and sometimes sugar are added and the whole mixture vigorously boiled for at least 1 hour.

Boiling is deemed essential to:
1. *Sterilise the wort* and kill off the enzymes still working in the malt which could upset the balance of sugars.
2. *Extract the flavour from the hops.* It takes one hour's vigorous boil to change the hop resins into bitterness.
3. *Removal of haze forming protein matter.* Boiling coagulates the excess protein matter so that the murky malt solution can end up as a crystal clear pint.

Is Boiling Really Necessary?

In the past I have always been a strong advocate of the need for efficient boiling based on my years of practical experience. I still hold firm on this belief. However, there are some beer kits based on

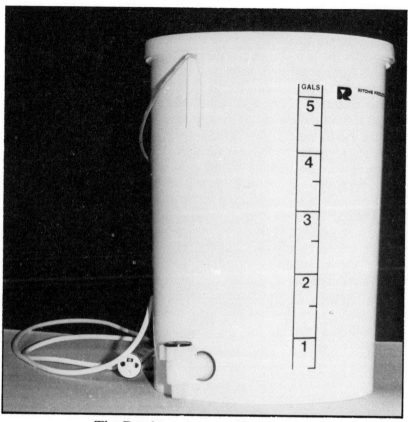

The Bru-heat, an excellent electric,
thermostatically controlled boiler.

malt extract (not the pre-boiled hopped wort type) where the brewing
instructions omit any boiling. Obviously the quality of the finished
beer must be satisfactory otherwise the kits would not sell. Boiling is
not the only criterion of quality beer production and kits can be
designed around it. Usually this means keeping the malt content low
to avoid haze problems. Referring to *malt extract* alone, unless the
recipe has been specifically designed as a "no boiling" brew, omitting
this stage courts disaster by encouraging infection and off flavours.
As discussed earlier, hopped worts can be employed in recipes to
by-pass the boiling stage if boiling does not fit in with your brewing
circumstances.

Sterilising the Wort

Concentrated malt syrups are usually pasteurised in the can and are thus supplied completely safe and sterile. Even when the larger cans are partially emptied, the degree of sugar concentration in the syrup is so strong that bacteria cannot survive in its presence. Diastatic malt syrups, however, are not pasteurised so as to preserve their enzymatic activity and some measure of boiling is essential here to kill off these enzymes before fermentation takes place.

Diluting the Extract

The thick viscous malt syrup must be diluted to form a more fluid solution before attempting to boil it. Syrupy solutions tend to burn on the boiler bottom, caramelising and adversely affecting the flavour. Ideally, 5 gallons of beer should be made from the same quantity of boiled wort.

However, boiling 5 gallons of wort requires a large boiler and the exercise produces copious supplies of steam. On the credit side, beers made with malt syrup diluted to their *original* density in the boiler produce finer flavoured beer devoid of the notorious "malt extract" tang. This aspect alone, makes the investment of a large boiler, such as the Bruheat, worthwhile. Using an extension lead the boiler can be positioned outside the back door to allow the steam to blow away.

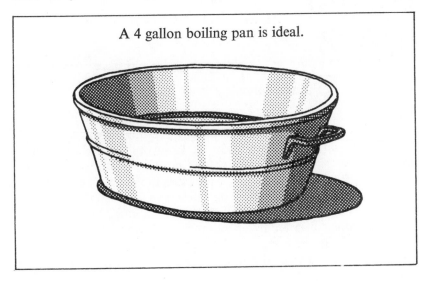

A 4 gallon boiling pan is ideal.

Problems With Small Boilers

Many home brewers own boiling pans, dixies and large saucepans of limited capacity. Attempting to boil up all the malt extract, a quantity of grain malts and a measure of hops can prove to be a really messy business. As the mixture approaches boiling point the contents erupt into a seething frothy mass. And if you are not careful it vents its wrath by boiling over on to the stove.

The obvious answer with a small boiler is to split the brew into two consecutive boils. Time is often at a premium with part-time brewers and prolonging the boiling just doubles the inconvenience. It will be useful here to discuss the parameters affecting the boiling process to decide the optimum system for your equipment.

Minimum Quantity for Boiling

The malt wort solution must be boiled vigorously and continuously. To achieve a nice rolling boil it obviously needs the solution to be as fluid as possible. Sometimes a really dilute wort suffers as well when the heat source is inadequate to maintain a vigorous boiling action. Insufficient dilution causes caramelisation, so we are looking for somewhere in between as a practical compromise. So much depends on the boiler shape, amount of dry grain and hops included that guidelines are only possible.

Weight of Ingredients (including extract, grain, hops and sugar)	Minimum Volume of Water for Boiling
1 lb.	4 pints
1 kg.	5 litres

Brewers with restrictive equipment will naturally try to cram everything into one boiling session if at all possible. However, there is nothing like practical experience for highlighting limitations and pitfalls and no doubt you will come to a satisfactory balance in the end.

Dividing A Brew for Boiling Purposes

Where the problem of limited boiling capacity must be overcome, a decision has to be made on how best to split the ingredients for the two boils. Technically, it is not desirable to divide the ingredients equally.

Typical recipes will call for the boiling of malt extract, dry roast grains, hops and water treatment salts. In the first boil include as much malt syrup as practicable (using recommendations above) and a measure of water treatment salts apportioned similarly. It is not essential to boil hops in this first stage since we are more interested in separating the unwanted protein matter. The action of the boiling wort will precipitate some of the hop resins as well as the protein and consequently can waste valuable hop goodness. On the other hand changing the resins to bitter tasting oils needs prolonged contact with boiling liquid and thus including some of the quota now ensures infusing adequate bitterness into the beer. Nearly all recipes recommend using two strains of hops, and if split boiling must be used, select half the "bittering" coarse hops and use them in the first boil.

After completing the initial boil, strain off the cooked wort into the intended fermenting bin. Return the hops used in the first boil back into the boiling pan. Add the remaining hops and malt extract, all the malt grains and balance of water treatment salts. Another decision to make. If you still have adequate freeboard in the boiler with all the second batch of ingredients inside, consider adding any sugar recommended by the recipe. Stir the contents to dissolve the malt extract and sugar before the temperature reaches boiling point. Boil vigorously as before and then strain off the liquid into the fermenting bin and mix with the first extraction of hopped wort.

Boiling Time

A newcomer to home brewing can easily be baffled by the inconsistency over the boiling time recommended in some recipes. Instructions call for boiling or simmering the hops with the malt solution for periods ranging from 20 minutes to 2 hours. What a difference! When you start thumbing through books and magazines for a suitable recipe to try, the simplicity of the method is a persuasive influence. Stating that the brew only requires minimum boiling will initially attract more of a following than if a vigorous 2 hour boil is called for. The truth is that a short boil will still turn out a reasonable beer, but a longer one will produce a much higher quality brew in every respect. You balance convenience against quality, which really sums up the whole approach to home brewing. Let's see what factors should influence our decisions.

Hop Flavour

The scalding boiling wort has contrary benefits to the hop. Boiling initiates the chemical change required to convert the soft Humulon resin into bitter tasting substances. Unfortunately, the mere action of boiling drives off the more volatile oils responsible for hop flavour and aroma.

The first minute or so of the boil sees the aromatic oils driven off followed closely over the next 10 minutes by the loss of the hop taste. A bitter flavour starts to predominate and 80 per cent of the alpha acid is converted in the following half hour. An hour's boil only extracts another 10 per cent.

To ensure that the finished beer has a balanced bitterness, hop flavour and aroma, the hops therefore should be added in stages. The bulk of hops are pitched in during the first half an hour and a smaller proportion (say 10 per cent) are saved and added 5 or 10 minutes before switching off. To try to capture some aroma and flavour with these late hops, I sometimes hold back half this quota and scatter them in immediately after switching off the boiler. In this way the essential oils are liberated into the wort, but not driven off.

Normally the loss of hop aroma is restored later by soaking a few dry hops in the casked beer. With the exception of a slight loss of goodness, all the necessary hop factors can be achieved within 1 hour's boil.

Wort Clarity

When malt wort is boiled the protein based matter in it becomes unstable. Initially the proteins cloud the wort as a fine grey mist. As boiling progresses, this finely dispersed matter clumps together, forming larger particles. Eventually the boiling solution separates as clear wort speckled with large particles of coagulated protein matter. On cooling, the degraded protein will settle out, so the clear wort can be strained off. If this coagulum is carried forward to the fermentation stage the beer will be prone to harsh flavours, poor fermentation and hazes.

The point when the boiled wort achieves complete gumming together of protein matter is referred to as the "hot break". Unless this point has been reached, crystal clear beer will not be possible. Undercooked worts display a detectable dullness when brewed. Obviously the clarity aspect is more pertinent to light coloured beer than dark brews.

57

I cannot state a definite time when this condition is met, as the change is more a function of the movement of the rolling boiling action rather than of time and temperature. The type of malt used also makes a difference. However, I would expect the hot break to be achieved with my recipes within an hour's boil.

Irish Moss

As clearing the wort can take longer than the extraction of hop flavour, any means of accelerating the hot break is welcome. Irish Moss, dried sprigs of special seaweed, added during the boil will in fact speed up the process. I would recommend adding 1 teaspoon of the sprigs to all recipes for light coloured brews.

> *Boiling the wort*
> One hour's vigorous boil should extract all the hop goodness and produce a hopped wort capable of being fermented into a high quality beer.

Pressure Cookers

Boiling under pressure reduces cooking time. Domestic pressure cookers can be used with advantage for small quantity brews.

Average size cookers can only cope with about 1½ lb. of malt syrup at a time. Boiling the wort under 15 lb./in.^{2} pressure will achieve a satisfactory hot break within 15 minutes. Because of the risk of hop debris choking and blocking the safety vent, I would recommend boiling the hops by themselves in an open topped vessel to extract flavour.

Boiling Hops Separately

Whole hop cones boiled in the malt wort help to hasten the hot break by their mechanical buffering action. Having said this, there are significant advantages for the home brewer in boiling some, if not all, his hops separately in tap water to which water treatment salts, such as Gypsum, have been added. Keeping the hop boil separate gives far better control of hop flavour.

Hop Boiling Bags

Hops can be boiled in special muslin bags simply to make straining off easier at the end. The bags tend to restrict the extraction of useful oils and resins. My recipes are based on the hops being boiled loose and hence the hoppiness could be a bit less if you are using these boiling bags. There is no advantage in easy straining if loose grains are boiled as well.

Boiling the Roast Grains

Straight malt extract recipes often incorporate crystal malt or dark roasted grains for flavour enhancement and colour. These adjuncts are crushed to expose their interior parts for efficient extraction. Commercial breweries coax these desirable characteristics out of the malt during the preliminary mashing stage. As we bypass this process, the malt must be dealt with during the boiling stage; a relatively coarse treatment compared with the gentle infusion method. Only a much smaller proportion of these grains are required in our brews and extraction is best carried out by pitching in the crushed malts during the last 10 minutes of the boil.

The redundant malt grains sink with the spent hops and assist with the formation of a filter bed to strain the clear wort off the precipitated protein matter. On the debit side, the grain absorbs and retains valuable extract and there is some merit in boiling them separately in water and straining off the liquid goodness straight into the fermenting bin.

Straining Off

Much of the benefits of boiling can be lost or destroyed by slack straining off. A well cooked malt extract wort will also contain a tremendous amount of redundant material. Spent hops (either whole cones or pellet fragments), malt grain husks and very flocculent greyish brown protein matter. All these items must be separated off the clear malt liquor. Natural cooling will deposit much of these substances within a few minutes of switching off the heat. So long as you are careful, most of the clear wort can be drained off (very slowly) through the tap of your boiler. Boiling pans do not have taps and the best method I have found is to simply strain off the solids through a fine sieve. Any absorbed extract left in the deposits can be retrieved by rinsing with a kettleful of hot water. The method is really quite inefficient and many undesirable substances pass to the collection vessel. Ideally the wort should be racked again as cooling throws a secondary deposit.

When boiling hop pellets in a malt wort I sometimes adopt another approach. After switching off, allow the debris to settle with cooling and then pour or strain off as much clear wort as possible. Then add some of the cold tap topping up water to the flocculent malt and hop debris and let it settle again. This time most of t⌐ 3 absorbed extract can be retrieved in the clear portion.

All collection vessels must be thoroughly sterilised before collecting wort.

Cooling the Wort

Following the straining off procedure, the wort should be cooled as rapidly as possible from its near boiling point to room temperature. Speed is desirable on two accounts. Firstly, the rich wort is a very attractive medium for growth of the wild yeasts and bacteria ever present in the atmosphere. We rely on our brewing yeast to produce alcohol quickly to kill them off. The delay period between cooling, pitching and production of alcohol can be long enough for the unwanted visitors to implant infection and off flavours. Secondly, the once bright, clear wort becomes dull and cloudy as it cools. Again the clouding is due to nitrogenous matter reverting to an insoluble state at low temperatures. The condition is known as the "cold break" and rapid cooling can lead to the precipitation of another light deposit. Racking off the cold break protein is especially desirable for lager beer production as this matter causes the notorious "chill haze" when beers are stored in the refrigerator.

Methods of Cooling

A fermenting bin full of very hot wort takes a long time to cool naturally. Some means of assisting the process is welcome. The obvious approach of trickling the hot wort from the boiler in a thin stream aerates as well as cools. Aeration provides oxygen to assist yeast growth. Alternatively, large bulks of hot wort can be forced cooled by standing the vessel in a sink or bath of cold water.

Home Made Wort Cooler

An easy made wort cooler uses a spiral of Microbore Central Heating Copper Tubing (length 10 m., bore 8 mm^2). The arrangement will cool down a wort to fermentation temperature in about 10 minutes.

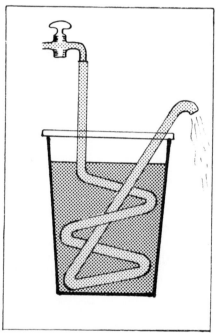

The copper tubing is best bent into a large spiral just big enough to drop into your wort vessel or boiler.

Topping Up

You will find that most recipes call for topping up the strained off boiled wort with water to make up the desired volume. Cold tap water is acceptable, but I would advise squirting in a small dose of sodium metabisulphite solution to chemically neutralise the chlorine present. Cooled water from the *hot* water tap will be chlorine free and thus can be used direct.

61

Where your domestic water supply is normally a bit discoloured or smells "earthy", I would strongly advise you to use only cooled *boiled* water, as these waters can contain wild yeasts and fungi capable of withstanding the chlorination and could taint your beer. Passing the water through a MAYREI Water Filter should help enormously as well.

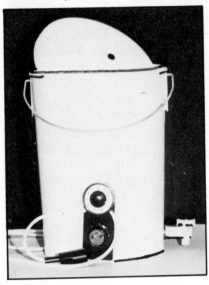

Bruheat Boiler

When brewing on a regular basis, it is worth investing in some custom built equipment. The Ritchie (Burton-on-Trent) Bruheat Boiler is certainly one useful item dealing with the boiling, mashing and even fermentation processes efficiently and under strict temperature control.

Basically, it is a 25 litre polypropylene bucket and lid which has a kettle type of heating element fitted in the side walls near the bottom. The element is controlled by a very sensitive simmerstat and is capable of keeping the temperature of the liquid inside to within a few degrees of its selected setting. Good for all stages of brewing.

Hydrometer (Beer Tester)

Home brewers find by experience that it is worth implementing some measure of quality control in their brewing. One small glass instrument called the hydrometer gives all the scientific insight to the progress of brewing needed for most recipes.

The HYDROMETER is simply a weighted glass float with a graduated scale indicating the relative density of the liquid in which it is immersed compared to water.

Unfermented beer is mainly a solution of sugar and is more dense than pure water. The more sugar (or malt extract) in the wort the denser the solution becomes. During fermentation, the yeast converts this sugar into less dense alcohol, thus the hydrometer will float high in the wort before fermentation and will gradually sink as the fermentation proceeds.

It is quite common for the instrument to have two or three scales on it. Our attention should be centred on the scale calibrated from 0.990 up to around 1.120. Unless the hydrometer has been specifically designed for beermaking, the scales of Potential Alcohol and Sugar Content can be misleading.

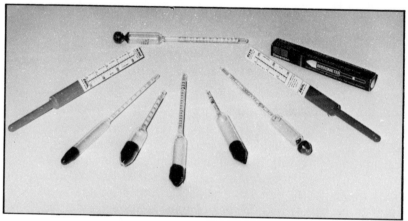

Popular hydrometers:
The shortest ones are solely for beer brewing.

Checking Specific Gravity
The scale 0.990 to 1.120 is a calibration of Degrees of Specific Gravity.

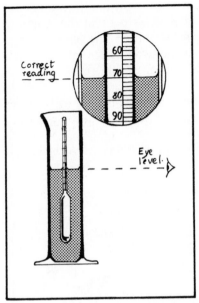

Correct
reading

Eye
level·

To check the reading, place the hydrometer into the beer and read off the figure against the scale making sure to compensate for the miniscus effect as illustrated in the accompanying diagram. Also spin the instrument to release clinging bubbles that could give extra buoyancy and a false reading.

Most of the recipes in this book give a figure of ORIGINAL GRAVITY; the reading taken in the wort immediately prior to fermentation. Checking this figure will indicate how well you have carried out the initial brewing stages. Normally, readings above the ones I quote should not be experienced, but I would expect your figures to be within two degrees of mine. Greater errors will need investigating to see just where valuable extract is being lost.

At the end of fermentation the specific gravity will normally fall below 1010 except where special body building ingredients are employed. The approximate amount of alcohol formed can be calculated from the following simplified equation:

$$\text{Alcohol Produced} = \frac{\text{Original Gravity} - \text{Final Gravity}}{7.5} \times 100\%$$

for example, consider a beer wort where the original gravity (O.G.) of 1036 ferments down to stable reading of 1006, then

$$\text{Alcohol} = \frac{1036 - 1006}{7.5} \times 100\%$$

$$= \frac{36 - 6}{7.5} \times 100\%$$

$$= 4.0\% \text{ Alcohol by Volume}$$

As stated above, beermaking hydrometers will give a direct reading of Alcohol Potential on line with Original Gravity marking.

Another point to remember is that hydrometers are normally calibrated to be correct at 15°C. Correction factors can be used for temperatures off this figure, but from my experience the calculations can be misleading. It is far better to cool a sample to room temperature and then take the reading.

SELECTING A YEAST

Fermentation marks the change from "wort" to "beer". Yeast introduced to the rich sweet wort acts on the sugar present and converts it into alcohol and carbon dioxide gas. As a living organism, Yeast must be handled with care and understanding to produce good beer. Choosing a good yeast is essential.

Yeast

Yeast is a low form of plant life and has the ability to multiply rapidly in sugar solutions, leaving in its wake the sugar split roughly into equal quantities of alcohol and carbon dioxide gas. In its natural wet state, yeast is a very unstable substance, so Home Brew yeasts are usually dried to give them better keeping qualities. Fresh brewery yeast will ferment a commercial beer wort down in 48 hours, whereas a dried home brew yeast will take at least twice as long to do the same job. As home brew customers we have a wide choice covering top and bottom fermenting strains, cultures, granules and even tablets of dried yeast. Top fermenters are employed in English ale brewing, whereas the rest of the world favour bottom fermenting strains for lager production.

Dried Beer Yeast

Each major supplier to the home brew trade markets a general purpose Beer Yeast under its own brand name. From my experience they all work acceptably well in our brews. There is not really very much to choose between them, a reasonable assumption, since some brands (not all) are supplied by the same bulk manufacturer! It is quite understandable that dehydration and freeze drying takes its toll of the living yeast cell count and some dried yeasts contain nutrients and yeast energisers to restore viability. The main advantages of dried yeasts are their availability and persistent, consistent performance over a wide range of room temperatures. They are not so tempermental as some of their thoroughbred cousins.

Dried Lager Yeast

Bottom fermenting yeasts are usually pure strains and are likely to give consistent fermentations devoid of off flavours.

Yeast Tablets

Compressing into tablet form retains all the attributes of the granules with possibly better keeping qualities.

Commercial Brewing Yeasts

I take every opportunity for getting a sample of genuine *fresh* brewery yeast. Pitched into home brews it makes an incredible difference to the performance of the fermentation and more important, the flavour of the finished beer. Really, it is hardly surprising. The success of brewing relies heavily on the quality of the yeast and no commercial brewery could afford to have anything less than the very best.

How to get a sample. I have made a point of arranging contacts to get samples direct from my local breweries. This course is not open to all, but other avenues are open. Your local public house carries ample stock to suit your needs. A bottle of Guinness Extra Stout is naturally conditioned and the yeast sediment can be cultivated for home use. Also many pubs serve "real ale"; naturally conditioned draught beer. The dregs of a quickly consumed cask contain enough healthy cells for our purposes. An arrangement with the landlord for collecting regular samples is worthwhile.

Genuine Yeast Cultures in liquid form can be purchased from the better home brew stockists. British Ale, Burton Beer, Stout and Danish Lager strains are particularly good.

Other Yeasts

If you are satisfied with the results of dried brewing yeasts, then it is worth experimenting with other strains. In common with many other brewers, I have found the results with General Purpose *Wine* Yeast and Allisons Baking Yeast surprisingly good.

Wine yeast, being a bottom fermenting strain that works naturally at room temperatures, is a very good alternative to lager yeast where a cooler environment for fermentation is difficult to maintain.

MAKING A YEAST STARTER

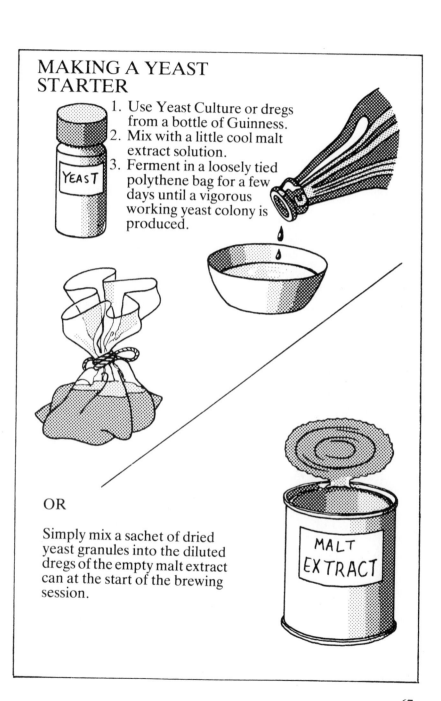

1. Use Yeast Culture or dregs from a bottle of Guinness.
2. Mix with a little cool malt extract solution.
3. Ferment in a loosely tied polythene bag for a few days until a vigorous working yeast colony is produced.

OR

Simply mix a sachet of dried yeast granules into the diluted dregs of the empty malt extract can at the start of the brewing session.

YEAST

MALT EXTRACT

Allinson's Baking Yeast seems to be a very active strain and does not impart any undesirable taints to the brew.

Yeast Starter

A yeast starter is simply a "mini-brew" made up sometime prior to the fermentation of the main batch of wort. The objects are to grow more yeast from a small sample and, or, to activate dormant dried granules. Getting the fermentation away to a fast start is essential. The pitched yeast should start to form a frothy layer over the wort surface *within a few hours* to protect it from airborne infection.

Yeast cultures and bottle sediments take a long time to create a visibly vigorous colony and hence must be set working a few days before the main brew. Instructions for using granulated yeasts often say that a starter is not needed, but I normally do make one. These should burst into action within half an hour of mixing and thus can be made up on the day of brewing. Normally I make up the yeast starter before getting down to the main brewing jobs.

YEAST NUTRIENTS

Fertilisers encourage plant growth and in the case of yeast we prefer to call it "Nutrients". Although beer worts are supposed to be adequately endowed with natural yeast food, the addition of yeast nutrients, Energisers and Purifiers always seem to improve fermentation.

Standard yeast nutrient preparations are mainly formulated from ammonium sulphate, diammonium phosphate and magnesium sulphate. On the other hand, energisers contain vitamins essential for yeast production. Combination preparations incorporating nutrients and vitamins obviously give the best of both worlds. With brewers in mind, one product includes a heading salt with its combined nutrient-energiser to ensure the beer produces ample and a long lasting foam head.

A yeast purifier and beer preservative as used by commercial breweries is now available to us and is a very welcome additive for keeping our home brew yeast fresh, viable and infection free.

These fermentation aids can be purchased in sachets, tubs and tablet form and all keep well in storage. To use, add the requisite dose when pitching in the yeast. Remember also, that a small pinch in the yeast starter helps to get the initial fermentation under way.

Our home brew beer worts are sometimes deficient in acid. Spooning in a scant ½ teaspoon of lactic or citric acid is beneficial, so long as these were not dosed in as water treatment. Too much acid gives beer a cidery flavour.

AN AIRLOCK . . .

is a simple one way valve. It allows the carbon dioxide gas liberated by the fermenting beer to escape before building up excessive pressure in its container. As the CO_2 pressure increases and becomes greater than that of the atmosphere, a bubble of gas is vented off through the water. When the fermentation has ceased, the water acts as a barrier and stops air coming in contact with the beer and spoiling it.

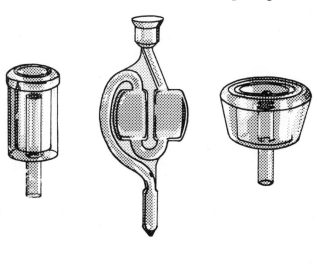

THE FERMENTATION

The initial fermentation in the plastic bin will take three to ten days depending on the strength of the brew, quality and type of yeast and the "cellar" temperature. Then there follows a very important stage of conditioning and clarification before the brew is matured in the bottle or cask.

We start with the plastic bin filled with the final quantity of sweet hopped wort and an activated starter.

The yeast starter should be pitched and roused into the wort immediately after the wort has cooled to room temperature (17°C.). Do not be hasty over pitching, as a premature pitching can scald the delicate cell yeasts and mar the whole fermentation progress. A thermometer is more reliable than dunking your finger in and proclaiming it as "cool enough"!

The yeast starts its job of breaking down the sugar into alcohol and carbon dioxide gas. The gas given off by the fermenting yeasts being much lighter than the dense environment in which it was formed, rises up through the wort in the form of bubbles. Sometimes the rising bubble takes along with it the yeast cell that initially produced the gas. On its way up to the surface it collides and combines with other like cells and forms a visible yeast projectile.

At the surface some of the bubbles burst to release the trapped gas. The remainder form a frothy mass that floats on the beer surface due to the buoyancy of the trapped gas. More and more yeast is sent up to pack on the surface as fermentation progresses and eventually the entire surface is covered with a light fluffy coating. Until this barrier is formed, the lid of the bin must be in place to protect the brew.

The initial yeast head purges the brew of unwanted debris and deposits it as speckles of dark brown matter on the foam. As the vigour of fermentation increases, a fountain like current is set up within the bin and most of this matter is deposited as peripheral scum on the inside walls at the level of the brew. Remove these waste products before they harden as brown scale or mix with the beer, ruining its flavour.

After about one day's fermentation the yeast crop can look quite frightening with long meringue-like tentacles of yeast protruding from the main crop.

The performance of the yeast after this reproductive peak marks the quality of the strain. So often the yeast crop vanishes to leave large oily bubbles floating on the beer. This is the hallmark of a weak yeast and occurs when granules and cultures have been stored too long or under the wrong conditions. Commercial yeasts which are used repeatedly weaken with age and can perform feebly as well. All brews should be roused daily to encourage fermentation.

A good dried granulated yeast will muster some yeast crop throughout fermentation although the covering will be pretty thin near the end. The more frail the yeast crop, the more vulnerable the brew becomes to infection, oxidisation and even contamination through contact with the spent brownish debris. In the latter stages snap on the lid to afford better protection.

A good commercial yeast will form a thick crust of yeast floating on the brew. Consequently it forms an effective barrier to the air and is inherently safer. The drawback with yeasts forming a pancake layer is that whilst sitting on top of the brew they cannot ferment it! Commercial strains need rousing two or three times daily to mix the yeast back into the beer. Use a long sterilised plastic spoon or paddle to swirl the brew against the underside of the yeast layer without actually breaking up the crop itself. As long as a yeast cap is present, leave off the lid of the bin. Air is beneficial to top fermenting yeasts and helps to avoid a sickly flavour sometimes experienced with enclosed brews.

The progress of fermentation can be monitored by taking daily readings with a hydrometer. A satisfactory attenuation is noted by a continual fall in the specific gravity reading. Initially the fall will be quite rapid and will slow down as the fermentation nears its end.

From My Brewery Log

Typical hydrometer readings during fermentation for a beer with an original gravity of 1.045:

Start	1045	
1st day	1042	
2nd „	1028	
3rd „	1016	
4th „	1010	
5th „	1007	
6th „	1006	
7th „	1006	Rack off now

As the fermentation slows down, the beer will start to clear from the surface. However this visual check may not herald the end of fermentation. The beer may have simply stopped working because the temperature is too cool, or the yeast may have failed.

Obviously it would be prudent to make some further checks. A hydrometer is a useful instrument here. To be safe for bottling, the specific gravity should be low in accordance with the guide-lines below and the brew should not be sweet in taste.

Checks for the End of Fermentation
1. Beer should not taste sweet.
2. There should be no noticeable fall in specific gravity readings over a 24 hour period.
3. The final S.G. reading should be less than one quarter of the original gravity figure.

Importance of Temperature

There is a natural, if not lazy attitude to home brew fermentations. We expect the yeast to fit into our modern home environment and to carry out its work at temperatures convenient to us. The poor yeast responds, but not as well as it could do if the temperature was adjusted right.

A true, healthy, top fermenting yeast performs best when kept to a temperature range of 14–17°C. (57–63°F.). Applied to commercial strains this is true, but our home brew yeasts work better in a range of 2–3°C. higher. Yeast activity increases with temperature and the extra heat compensates in some ways for the relatively small quantity we pitch in.

Lager Yeast

There is one very big difference between the top and bottom working strain of yeast used for lager production. And that is the temperature of fermentation. Lager yeast should be fermented much lower around 7–10°C. (45–50°F.) to get the *true* lager flavour. The problems this creates in home brewing will be discussed later.

A Constant Temperature

Yeast works much better in a constant temperature enviro..ment. Fluctuations causing alternate slowing down and racing of the fermentation will prove troublesome. Normally home brews are

72

conducted in places where it creates the least inconvenience to the rest of the household. Cupboards under the stairs, spare bedrooms, lofts, garages and garden sheds are favourite sites. A centrally heated house affords more temperature stability than an outhouse. Brewing bitters, lights, milds and other English brews we need heat during the colder seasons and some means of cooling for lager production in the summer months.

Dealing with the Cold

Domestic dwelling houses are warmed by central heating or individual direct fires. For localised quick, direct heat, fires are best, but for overall comfort most people prefer the central heating system. Much of this reasoning applies to the needs of yeast, in so much that we can construct a house, or more correctly, a "fermentation cupboard", or use one of the many individual heating elements especially designed for home brewing.

I use an old wardrobe as a fermentation cupboard. It is insulated inside with polystyrene tiles and heated with a small thermostatically controlled tubular heater. Such a big cupboard can deal with six full size brews (over 100 litres) in various stages of fermentation, conditioning and maturation. The running costs of electricity are minimal. If you contemplate copying my arrangement then get a qualified person to install the electrical equipment. Alternatively a fermentation cupboard can be heated using one of the larger sized home brew heaters permanently installed in a fermenting bin filled with water.

I like the custom built heaters for their efficiency, safety and simplicity. They come in various guises as is shown on page 74.

Thermal Belt

Thermal belts are electrically heated cables or straps for wrapping around the outside of the plastic bin and should be positioned near the base for maximum effect. The Brewbelt is a continuously energised one and supplies a large area of warmth to the bin.

Another wrap around system uses a new cable heater made from special material that controls its own heat output in response to changes in temperature. As the temperature falls the electrical current increases to dissipate more heat. Conversely the heat output decreases as the temperature rises. This self regulating feature is very reliable and economic.

TYPES OF FERMENTATION HEATER

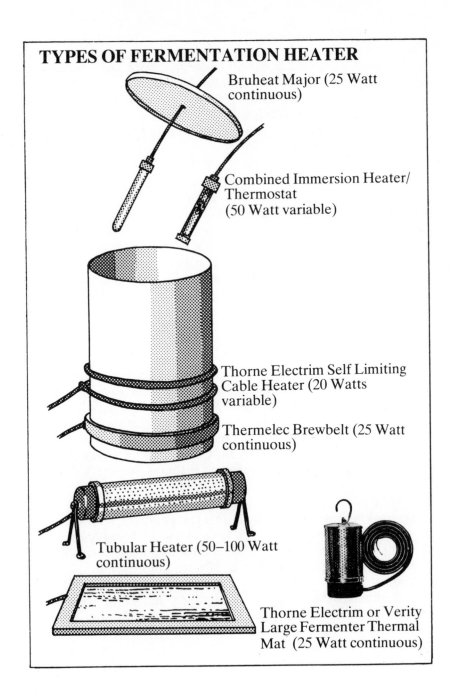

Bruheat Major (25 Watt continuous)

Combined Immersion Heater/ Thermostat (50 Watt variable)

Thorne Electrim Self Limiting Cable Heater (20 Watts variable)

Thermelec Brewbelt (25 Watt continuous)

Tubular Heater (50–100 Watt continuous)

Thorne Electrim or Verity Large Fermenter Thermal Mat (25 Watt continuous)

Base Heaters

Base heaters were primarily designed for using with 1 gallon demijohn jars. The four jar size called the Electrim Large Fermenter or Verity Tray fits beneath most brewers bins. Again the element is continuously rated and is placed in the best position for heat transfer.

Immersion Heaters

There are many immersion heaters for home brewing based on the fish tank heater principle. The elements ranging from 50 watt to 200 watt are housed in a sealed glass test tube. Some versions have integral thermostats to give a measure of temperature control. Preset to 75°F. or 85°F., the thermostat can be altered if required. It is essential for the heating bulb to be suspended in mid-brew to prevent localised heat damaging the plastic container.

The Bruheat Major is simply a long nylon covered rod that prevents the beer coming into contact with the heating elements metal housing. Continuously rated at 25 watts it is virtually indestructible.

REMEMBER TO CHECK THE TEMPERATURE WITH A THERMOMETER TO ENSURE THE HEATING ELEMENT IS KEEPING THE BULK OF THE BREW BETWEEN 16°–21°C. (60°–70°F.).

LAGER FERMENTATION

Real lager is the most difficult style of beer to imitate. The traditional method calls for cool fermentation and a prolonged storage at near freezing temperature. Commercial breweries would not follow these demanding processes if the true lager flavour could be achieved without them. How well we fare depends largely on how far we are prepared to follow these practices.

English style lager is much simpler and follows closely to normal home brew methods, hence success is assured.

At this juncture, we are only interested in the fermentation stage of lager production.

Lager yeast should be kept within a temperature range 0°–10°C. throughout the fermentation and lagering process. The recommendation applies to genuine cultures and dried granules. Really it should be a demand rather than a recommendation.

Low temperature fermentation is essential to stop lager yeast developing flavours not conducive to the true lager taste.

Lager yeast should not be fermented at normal room temperatures. This doesn't mean the yeast will not work in a warmer environment. In fact it reacts very vigorously and ferments the brew out as efficiently as most top fermenting strains. The drawback is simply that the taste is not so good.

Not all strains of lager yeast are doomed to failure as I suggest. It is worth experimenting with different brands and also trying general purpose wine yeast for lager brews.

The practical problems of cool fermentation are not easy. Warming a brew by ten degrees is much easier than cooling it by the same amount. Not only should the fermentation be cool, but it should be constant. An even temperature is more important here than in top fermenting brews. Storing the brew for *many* weeks at just above freezing point was the traditional way of clearing the brew of the protein matter responsible for chill haze. Fluctuations in temperature slow down or inhibit this process. Thus the success of fermenting lager brews in outside garages or sheds must be limited by changes in the ambient air temperature.

Use Old Refrigerator

Refrigeration is the best method of temperature control for lager beer production. Buying a refrigerator just for brewing is not so extravagant as it first may seem. A second-hand small refrigerator can be purchased for about half the price of a pressure barrel and is a good investment for all your brewing needs. The freezer compartment will prove ideal for keeping all your hops in cold storage. The main cubicle can house yeast samples and finings. To ferment your lager place the brew in a square polythene cube within the main chest area. Check with a thermometer to find the dial setting which averages a temperature of 7°C. (45°F.). The primary fermentation will take about two weeks at this temperature. After racking, the brew can be returned to the refrigerator and the dial setting taken down a notch to mature the brew around 4°C. During the next four to six weeks the brew acquires the mature crispness peculiar to lager.

After brewing lager using refrigeration you prove the simplicity of the method and the futility of trying to improvise these techniques.

LAGER THE EASY WAY

The obvious approach to lager brewing is to try first the easy recipes designed to make the process similar to normal ale brewing. Special lager malt extracts, judicious selection of a suitable yeast and employing flaked maize and rice all help in this respect. The results are brews flavoured like some English lagers. Dissatisfaction can then only be overcome by resorting to the refrigerated techniques.

SAVING YEAST

Once you have found a good sample of yeast, try saving it for subsequent brews. The best time to collect some is during the fermentation by selecting a spoonful or two from beneath the yeast cap. The clean, fairly well drained sample is placed in a small polythene bag, with if possible, a pinch of yeast preserver and steriliser. Secure reasonably firm with an elastic band and store in the *cool* chest compartment of the refrigerator.

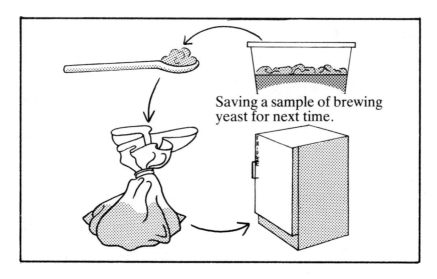

Saving a sample of brewing yeast for next time.

CLEARING THE BEER

The young beer at the end of fermentation is not ready for immediate bottling or casking. A secondary settling stage is advised to clear the brew of surplus yeast. The beer is racked into vessels affording airlock protection to ensure it rests under sterile conditions and where finings and other adjustments can be made to enhance the performance and quality of the poured drink.

Between fermentation and the final storage in bottles or barrel, the beer undergoes the most crucial period in its life. Bottling too soon, besides being a dangerous practice, will certainly result in yeasty, cloudy, poor flavoured beer. Playing safe by leaving the brew to stop working completely risks contamination through contact with air. It would be nice to be able to filter the brew bright as achieved in commercial breweries, but as yet filtering is not quite so easy for us.

Finings

The age old method of clearing beer is to use prepared additives called finings to accelerate the natural processes. Two types are available, both chemically related, and both glutinous animal products.

Gelatine

Gelatine should be used in the same context as a coarse filter since it is the best method of clearing the really cloudy beer found at the end of fermentation. Some manufacturers sell Gelatine by name or as DRY BEER FININGS and another common source is as the household preparation "Davis Gelatine". It comes in $\frac{1}{2}$ oz. sachets (15 gm.). The dried granules must be dissolved in water heated from cold. Stir continuously in $\frac{1}{2}$ pint of water to dissolve the gelatine before the mixture boils. The hot liquid should be added direct to the beer and *thoroughly* stirred in. It will clear a racked beer star-bright within a day.

Another advantage with Gelatine is that it can be added at the onset of fermentation. Its presence does retard fermentation somewhat by making the yeast sink to the bottom, but twice daily rousing soon disperses the yeast again to maintain attenuation. Once fermentation nears its end the fining action clears the brew, creating the possibility of bottling the brew straight from the bin. The gelatine's action is not restricted by constraints of temperature which prove troublesome with its rival Isinglass.

Isinglass

In its natural form Isinglass is a mass of fine white hair manufactured from the dried stomach of the sturgeon fish. These thin shreds are dissolved in acid solutions to form a glutinous paste sold to us as LIQUID BEER FININGS.

The object of isinglass based finings are to settle out the small amount of yeast present and necessary in casks of draught beer for conditioning purposes. Trying to clear yeast saturated beer with isinglass is a hopeless task.

Liquid finings must be kept cool to be effective as temperatures above 20°C. will cause them to go "slack" and be useless for fining. The fining action is also dependent on temperature. For some odd reason, these finings must be added to the beer *on a rising temperature* for them to act efficiently. Normally this means dosing them in early in the morning after the cold of the night and before the heat of the day.

Some variations are worth noting. The Cordon Brew type incorporates a starch enzyme for dealing with any residual starch left in the finished beer. "Two in Harmony" and others are a two pack arrangement consisting of auxiliary finings as well as the normal isinglass. The combination gives a better fining action. Isinglass's ability to aid clarification relies on an electrical phenomenon of neutralising electrical charges. Auxiliary finings are mixed in first to set up the right charge conditions before the main ones are introduced

Keep all liquid beer finings in the refrigerator when not required.

HOW WE CARRY OUT THE RACKING AND CLARIFICATION DEPENDS ON THE BREWING EQUIPMENT WE USE AND THE NEEDS OF THE BEER BEFORE BOTTLING AND CASKING. CONSIDER THE FOLLOWING OPTIONS.

Method 1:
Clearing in the Fermenting Bin. The simplest method of all. Many home brewers who only possess the bare essentials such as fermenting bin and bottles or a pressure barrel must adopt this procedure because all other ways call for another or other vessels giving the same capacity to accommodate the racked beer.

When the beer has finished in the fermenting bin, skim the surface of all surplus yeast and wipe clean any peripheral scum at the surface of the brew.

Crush two Campden tablets and stir into the brew. These are a source of sulphur dioxide and as such act as an anti-oxidant, preservative and a means of knocking out any residual yeast still working. The effect wears off in a couple of days so clarification must be completed in this period. Adding beer finings to the dosed beer helps enormously. Snap on the bin lid tightly and leave undisturbed whilst clearing takes place.

Method 2:
Rack and Rack again. Yeast will drop out of solutions of beer quite quickly to form a sediment especially when allowed to stand in a cool place. Using two fermenting bins the brew can be transferred from one to another by racking off the sediment as it forms. Racking daily two or three times is usually sufficient to clear the brew.

The big danger with successive racking is the risk of undue aeration and all the problems that it brings. Adding three crushed Campden tablets and finings to the first racking offsets this risk to such a degree that it is well worth considering. Remember to keep the lid on tight during the rest periods.

Method 3:
Rack, Rest and Adjust. Malt extract consists of totally fermentable maltose and a smaller proportion of unfermentable dextrins. Between these extremes is a group of partially fermentable sugars which keep the fermentation ticking over. Even after the hydrometer readings appear steady and fermentation in the bin is deemed finished, a small number of persistent bubbles rise to the surface, showing some yeast activity is still going on. Called secondary fermentation, it is not enough to throw a protective blanket of CO_2 over the brew, but sufficient to aggravate the clarification process.

Whilst these partially fermentable sugars are being used up it is advisable to rack the beer into gallon jars or a large polythene cube fitted with airlocks. Rack the beer off the sediment in the fermentation bin and fill each recipient vessel, leaving a bit of room for the finings.

Adding Gelatine Finings

The made up $\frac{1}{2}$ pint solution should be added to the beer before it cools. If the secondary fermentation is still brisk wait a day or so before preparing and stirring in the finings. Swirl and mix for at least *two minutes* to disperse them efficiently.

The most convenient container for holding 5 gallons of racked beer is a 25 litre polythene cube. Rinse out and sterilise first before filling with beer. Add the finings, replace the cap and check the tap is closed before swirling the cube to mix the contents. Position the cube with its tap uppermost and vent off the build up of gas. An airlock must be fitted. A most effective airlock can be made by inserting a length of rubber tubing over the tap outlet and immersing the other end in a bottle half filled with water. Remember to open the tap to vent the CO_2 gas given off by the secondary fermentation through the water. Another technique is to prise out the tap from the filler cap and plug the hole with a standard rubber bung and airlock. Because the cube is flexible, I would advise only using the VINTRAP type of airlock which has been designed to prevent air being sucked back into the cube when changes in ambient temperature occur.

A polypin is sufficiently translucent to see how clear the beer is. After a day nearly all the yeast should be deposited as a thick sediment. However creases in the side walls of the polypin act as ledges to collect the falling sediment and these need prodding to release their catch. Another day should see the beer starbright.

The beer can be left for weeks in this condition if required. The decision rests mainly on the quality of the yeast. Unless it is really sound, "yeast bite" will occur resulting in a very harsh acid taste imparted to the beer through the decomposition of dead yeast cells. We have the choice of racking the brew again into a fresh container or simply carrying on with the standard bottling or casking procedures. Normally, any brew can be left in this state for a week before the flavour deteriorates.

ADDING GELATINE FININGS

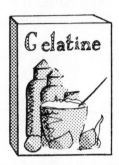

Making up finings by dissolving sachet contents in warm water.

Racked beer awaiting final topping up with Gelatine Solution.

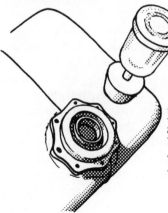

Using Polypin 25 litre cube

Prise out tap from filler cap and fit airlock and bung. Use VINTRAP type of airlock which operates on a pressure vent principle.

At this point it is worth sampling the brew using a drinking straw to assess whether any adjustments are needed before going any further.

Clarity, head retention, bitterness, sweetness and colour can be altered now, but adjustments must be implemented on a sediment free bulk.

QUALITY CONTROL

Before its fate is sealed in the bottle or barrel, a mediocre brew can be transformed by adjusting the bitterness, hop flavour, sweetness and its appearance using some of the many aids to beer quality available to us.

It makes sense to carry out any alterations to the beer character and flavour whilst you have the chance to do so. There are so many variables in the brewing process and the ingredients that some means of "tuning in" is very desirable. My tastes govern my approach to brewing and thus my recipes will reflect my palate preferences. The object of the book is to create beers that you like, and just on this score, minor adjustments should be considered as normal practice.

Preparing the Beer

Before adjustments are made the beer must be sediment free simply for practical considerations. Mixing in some additive would only stir up any deposit present. All I do is to siphon the beer off the sediment in the polypin into another. About ½ pint is stood aside for analysis.

Bitterness

Roll a mouthful of beer around your tongue for a few seconds before swallowing to assess bitterness. The degree of sensation depends on the amount of carbon dioxide gas in solution. A gassy beer tastes more bitter than a flat one. Ours at this stage will be virtually flat and so we must err on the light side.

Cautiously add *isomerised hop extract* to increase the bitter taste. Even resorting to dispensing with an eye dropper would not be amiss here as the extract is highly concentrated. A rough guide to the dosage could be made by adding drops to a drawn off pint. It is easier to mix evenly here and the total requirement is a simple multiple of the pint dose.

Hop Flavour

Much of the hop flavour is lost in the boiling process and is sometimes restored in commercial draught beers by adding a handful of dry hop cones to the casks before it reaches the pub. The flavour is soaked out and the redundant cones are held back in the barrel by perforated holes on the backside of the tap. In a home brew draught beer reckon on two whole cones for each gallon. Some means of filtering them out is required before they plop into your beer glass. Two methods shown below work quite well.

HOP FILTERS FOR BARRELS

Nylon scouring pad jammed in tap aperture

OR

Perforated polythene tube with wine cork plug

Hop Tea

Cover a small handful of hops with boiling water and strain off the infusion after a few minutes. Alternatively use hop pellets.

Sprinkle Hop Pellets

Powder the pellets between thumb and forefinger straight into the brew. Just like mother does with a meat cube. Use one pellet per gallon.

The powder debris settles out after about one week's soak and thus should not be inadvertently transferred to the bottles or barrel. An interesting variation is to mix the powdered pellets with the gelatine finings and use in the first racking.

Hop Aroma

All the dry hopping techniques help to restore the hop bouquet. Any additional aroma required can be introduced by adding a few *drops* of *Essential Oil of Hops*.

Head Retention

A nice lacing of foam is visually enticing and primes the senses for enjoying the glass of beer. Brown ales, stouts, lager and any bottled beer for that matter look quite ridiculous without their foam head. I cannot be a purist over this matter. If people prefer to see a nice frothy head on their beer then give it to them. Artificial heading agents give reliable consistent performances. Natural head forming substances in beer are destroyed in the presence of even the minutest trace of household washing up liquids and detergents. The substitute extracts are completely stable and overcome this problem.

Heading Powder

The M.E.B. type available to us is the standard heading compound used in commercial breweries and mixes well into the beer before casking. Do not double dose it after using the yeast nutrient and combined heading salt during the fermentation stage. For no other reason than habit, I prefer heading powders for draught beers and the liquid variety for bottled brews.

Heading Liquid

Telling you that Heading Liquids are made from Aquilia bark or Yucca Mohauenis extracts means little more than the fact I have read the label and you haven't yet! 1 teaspoon (5 ml.) is sufficient dosage for 5 gallons of beer.

Colour

Brewer's caramel or even gravy browning (also caramel) are used to increase the colour of beer. Sometimes referred to as beer colouring, the very thick, intensely dark compound of burnt sugar must be diluted first. Dissolve a sticky spoonful in boiling water and stir until an even colour is reached. Mix it into the beer a spoonful at a time until the right shade is achieved.

Sweetness

Home brewed beer tends to have an inherent harshness not associated with commercial equivalents. Whether it is because ours are naturally conditioned and theirs is normally pasteurised, I am not sure. Probably both reasons are contributory.

Adding a small amount of artificial sweetening makes all the difference to most of our beers; especially the young and immature ones. 1 saccharin tablet per gallon of beer smooths out the roughness without imparting a detectable sweetness. (Think how little sweetness 1 tablet would bring to a gallon of tea or coffee).

For accurate dispensing I prefer to use Sweetex Liquid where 4 drops impart the equivalent taste of a teaspoonful of sugar. The formulation for these sugar substitutes vary enormously especially with the powder or granulated varieties and hence it pays to experiment to find the one best suited to your palate. Wine sweetener gives good results as well.

Sweet stouts, brown ale and other brews require a sweet taste as part of their character. Now is the time to make these adjustments before the sweetness of the priming sugars confuses matters. Lactose is particularly recommended as it does not leave a distinctive bitterness sometimes found with a saccharine substance. Dissolve thoroughly first.

Malt Flavour

Increasing the malt flavour is a much neglected technique. The fresh flavour and aroma of the malt can be extracted from an infusion with the crushed grain. To perk up your brew select the same type of grain used in the basic recipe. For example, crystal malt in bitters, pale ales and lights and roast barley, black or chocolate malt for dark ales.

Crush a small handful of the grain, place in a pan and cover with boiling water. Simmer for not more than *2 minutes* and strain off through a fine sieve. When cool the infused extract can be mixed in where it will increase *colour* as well as flavour.

Clarity

Where the clarity of the brew is suspect and a doubt exists over its ability to fall bright during maturation, a few tests are worthwhile.

To check whether suspended yeast is the problem, rack off a sample into a clear "dry ginger ale" bottle. Prime and store in a warm place and as pressure builds up in the bottle, the beer will be seen to start clearing from the surface. Not much, really, but enough to prove the whole batch will clear in time.

If the beer clears when the temperature goes up then the clouding is due to protein haze. The remedy is to use CHILL HAZE RE-MOVER which when introduced as recommended on the instructions will deposit all the harmful matter. A side effect is a partial removal of the natural head forming constituents in the beer. A measure of heading liquid offsets this loss.

A dull wort could result from unconverted starch being carried through the fermentation stage. This condition should only arise where mashing is adopted in a recipe. Again the defect can be overcome. Enzyme preparations such as DIASTASE or FUNGAL AMYLASE will degrade this residual starch and clear the brew. At normal storage temperatures the reaction could take up to two weeks to complete.

PRIMING

Priming is the term for the rekindling of fermentation to give life and sparkle to bottled beers and condition to draught ales. Sugar is added to the beer and from its reaction with the yeast the carbon dioxide liberated dissolves back into the brew creating the characteristic fizziness and frothy foam head.

We know that yeast converts sugar into alcohol and carbon dioxide gas and it is this latter natural by product which carbonates our beer. Also we appreciate that the gas must be under some degree of pressure in the bottle for the poured drink to perform correctly.

The preceding fermentation and settling stages leave the beer flat and devoid of any measure of dissolved carbon dioxide gas. To restart the fermentation in the bottle we must have sugar and a little yeast present. The amount of gas produced is critical and must be carefully controlled to avoid excessive build up of dangerous gas pressure.

Gas Pressure

The pressure of gas in beer is not usually referred to as lb./in² or kp./cm² but in "volumes". One volume is the amount of gas in a bottle or cask at standard room temperature and atmospheric pressure. Thus "two volumes" of gas will create twice atmospheric pressure.

Bottled beers normally contain 1.2 to 1.6 volumes of carbon dioxide gas. Calculations now can be based on the practical assumption that 3 oz. of sugar yields 5 gallons of CO_2 gas (or 4 gm. gives 1 litre).

By utilising this information, the following priming rates have been calculated assuming the sugar used is entirely fermentable and that a little residual malt sugar is available in the beer to help as well.

PRIMING FOR BOTTLED BEERS
1 pint bottle use $\frac{1}{2}$ teaspoon ($2\frac{1}{2}$ ml.)
1 litre bottle use 1 teaspoon (5 ml.)

Draught Beers

Priming in draught brews warrants other considerations because the sugar is added for flavour balance as well as for producing conditioning gas. In bottled beers we wait until all the primings have worked out before drinking it, whereas draught beers are tapped whilst some sugar is still in solution and only a little has been converted to gas. The low gas content and residual sweetness are characteristic of draught ales. In effect we are drinking the brew prematurely.

The amount of sugar added is judged mainly from the flavour aspect and due regard must be taken of the dispensing system. Gassy beers, backed by CO_2 injector units are best kept less sweet than the real ale style.

PRIMING FOR DRAUGHT BEER
3 oz./5 gallons real draught ale 100 gm./25 litre
2 oz./5 gallons if CO_2 injector used 60 gm./25 litre

Since the flavour of the priming sugar is important with draught beers, then consider using other choices than the plain white household type. Brown sugar, Demerara and Barbados are particularly good as direct substitutes.

As we drink draught beer in the throes of fermentation, attention must be given to minimising yeast clouding. A method I employ is to use brewing sugar syrup, golden treacle or lumps of glucose chips. In their natural state, without dissolving first as a more dilute solution, they display a limited surface area for the yeast to feed on.

Consequently a slow consistent secondary fermentation is achieved and with the help of finings, the beer stays clear. When I rack a particular clear brew into the barrel and suspect the yeast may take a long time to build up again, a few granules of dried yeast are sprinkled neat on to the brew or golden syrup added as primings.

Krausen

"Krausening" refers to a very effective system of priming beer with a small quantity of wort taken from a freshly fermenting brew. 1 pint of wort from a like brew taken within the first day of fermentation contains a very active yeast and malt sugar, and will prime a 5 gallon brew.

Alternatively, draw off a pint of the hot wort after brewing and put aside in a refrigerator. Ferment the bulk as usual and introduce the unfermented wort when casking. This is my favourite method for fresh flavour and efficient priming.

Fungal Amylase

An interesting technique for priming relies on the sugar already in the beer. Theoretically all the available sugar will have been utilised by the yeast. However, all beers still contain some sugar not capable of being fermented by yeast. Certain enzyme preparations, Fungal Amylase, the only one available to us, has the ability to break down some resistant dextrins into fermentable sugars.

The reaction is slow and offers the advantages of slow conditioning and improved clarity. A priming solution can be made with the malto-dextrin "body builder" powder. Dissolve the same quota as sugar priming in boiling water. When cool mix in 1 teaspoon of Fungal Amylase before adding to the beer.

More simply, add the enzyme direct to the beer and rely on it feeding on the Dextrinous sugars already present.

Priming in Bulk

In the previous discussion on improving beer quality, many adjustments and additives are suggested before the brew is bottled or casked. There is no reason why the adding of the priming sugar cannot be done then as well. Simply dissolve the requisite amount in boiling water first and stir thoroughly into the beer when cool.

BOTTLING

Bottling beer is a convenient means of reducing the brew to manageable proportions. Proper beer or cider bottles in sound mechanical condition can be reused, filled and sealed with the help of special crown caps, closures and applicators. Other bottles in general domestic use may be suitable recipients for our beer if their limitations are accepted.

All home brewed beer must in essence be naturally conditioned and it is this type of beer that has always been reckoned to possess the finest flavour. Conditioning in the bottle implies that secondary fermentation will continue due to the action of yeast on the residual sugar in the beer, formed naturally or by added primings. The gas liberated by this action is trapped in the bottle and some dissolves in the beer.

When the bottle is opened after a suitably long maturation, and poured, the release of gas brings sparkle and zest to the drink and a desirable briskness to the palate as well as promoting a nice frothy head over the surface.

Bottles

Obviously it is preferable to rely solely on genuine beer bottles as these are designed to withstand the internal pressure generated inside. Until you have mastered the technique of bottling home brew and understood through practical experience the implications of over priming and the dangers of excessive gas pressures in beer, you would be advised to use only these proper ones. Beer bottles can be purchased new in home brew shops or saved after consuming the contents of commercial brews.

However, once you have accepted the responsibility of not endangering yourself or others through over priming, there is a whole host of suitable bottles in general domestic use suitable for keeping our beer. Any bottle which has held carbonated fizzy drinks should be safe enough for us. In this group I include lemonade bottles (even the new plastic ones), mixer drinks and colas. Mind you, these may be convenient containers, but aesthetically they leave a lot to be desired.

Standard British Beer Bottle

Plastic Reseal Cap

Metal Crown Cap

Traditional Screw Stopper
Beer Bottle

Insert Pad

Lemonade Bottle

External Screw Cap

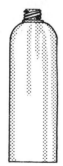

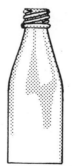

New Plastic Lemonade and
Cola Bottle.

⅓ rd pint Mixer Drink Bottle

Pouring a brown ale from a coke bottle creates immediate suspicion as to the contents! Nearly all are clear glass or plastic where the contents are on view. The advantage is in seeing when the beer is clear and ready for drinking, but exposure to sunlight can deteriorate the beer and hence these bottles should be stored in the dark.

Closures

Lemonade bottles sometimes have "use once" seals in the cap which damage easily and cannot be relied on to maintain pressure. New caps and insert seals are available in the better home brew shops with all the other types needed.

Plastic Reseals

Plastic reseal caps replace the metal crown caps on standard beer bottles. They are simply pushed on to seal the neck of the bottle. A small tag on the side assists with removal. Although advertising legalities prevent them saying so, I have found these caps may be used many times without failure.

Screw Stoppers

Internal stoppers are being replaced universally by crown caps. There are still plenty of the quart flagons about with screw tops which are much sought after by home brewers for their size and convenience.

External Screw Caps

So many people are now using lemonade and cola bottles for brewing that spare caps and insert seals are regular stock items now in home brew shops.

The popular external screw cap.

Crown Caps

Crown Caps on our bottles of home brew give that professional touch. The metal caps have serrated edges which are crimped on to the bottle neck using special applicator tools. These range from a simple Crown Capper, a female punch that needs to be hammered to impress the metal caps on, to the lever operated types and bench models. I think the investment of one of the latter types is well worth while. The lever action is self locating to crimp the caps on accurately and its action is smooth, involving no potentially dangerous impacting.

Beerbrite Caps

The big drawback with naturally conditioned beers is the yeast sediment in the bottle. Beerbrite caps have a large blister where the offending yeast can be collected and removed. Crystal clear beer may be drawn off right down to the last drop in the bottle. Taking off the yeast gives tremendous control of quality as it is only the continual contact with the sediment which eventually deteriorates the beer flavour. Once the Beerbrite Cap has been removed the maturation process is arrested and the beer maintains its peak of condition and quality. The technique has obvious advantages for Beer Competition work.

Using Beerbrite Caps

Prime and bottle as normal and then fit the Beerbrite Caps. Store the beer in a warm place to encourage the yeast to ferment out the priming sugar. After a few days the sedimentary yeast must be coaxed into the cap by inverting the bottle. Special Angle Brackets are available for this purpose or you can improvise with any method that supports the weight of the bottle off the plastic blister. I use a segregated wine bottle cardboard box. The box is supported above

BOTTLING ACCESSORIES

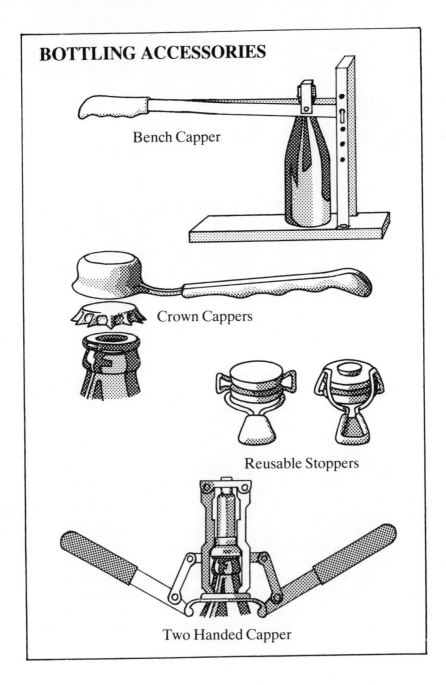

Bench Capper

Crown Cappers

Reusable Stoppers

Two Handed Capper

the ground and each partition has a hole punched in it so that the Beerbrite Cap can protrude through. Twist each bottle daily to assist the depositing of yeast. Once the yeast is all in the blister, bend the cap in half and secure in position with the wire provided. The yeast is now separated from the rest of the beer.

The Beerbrite Cap is not very attractive and can be replaced if desired with a crown cap or plastic reseal. Chill the beer in the refrigerator for a few hours before swapping the closures.

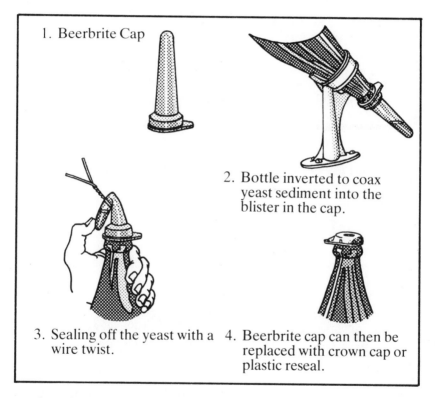

1. Beerbrite Cap

2. Bottle inverted to coax yeast sediment into the blister in the cap.

3. Sealing off the yeast with a wire twist.

4. Beerbrite cap can then be replaced with crown cap or plastic reseal.

Bottling the Brew

Collect enough bottles for the capacity of beer to be bottled. Check and inspect them for chips and cracks that would impair their mechanical strength. Reject any suspect ones. Make certain all the closures are in good order especially regards the sealing washers or inserts.

Sterilise Everything

Line up all the bottles and funnel half a bottle of stock sterilising solution from one to the other. After the last bottle, empty the solution into a jug. From here give the syphon tube, funnel and spoon the sterilising treatment as well. Finally tip in all the closures, soak awhile and then discard the liquid. Drain each bottle thoroughly and flick the last drips out. There is no need to rinse out.

CLEAN BOTTLES

It is sometimes difficult to see if the inside of dark brown or green beer bottles are clean.

Fill the bottle with water and hold up to the light. Even minute deposits are clearly shown up by the illuminating and magnifying power of the water inside.

Priming and Beer Treatment

The beer for bottling should have already benefitted from your considered attention. First of all it should be as clear as a poured pint. Maybe also it will be already primed, dosed with heading liquid and the like prior to bottling and thus you can just carry on with the rest of the process. The other option is to prime and implement other beer treatment now and I will discuss these techniques.

Priming Sugar

White or brown sugar must be in granulated or powdered form for ease of funnelling into each bottle. Dose every bottle with $\frac{1}{2}$ teaspoon per pint of sugar or pro rata for other sizes.

Yeast

It would be unusual for any home brew beer at this stage not to contain sufficient viable yeast cells to promote bottle fermentation, even though the brew has been fined and appears crystal clear. To ensure conditioning gets off to a good start I often *yeast* prime the beer as follows. Cream a little yeast, sugar and water in an egg cup and stand in a warm place for ten minutes or so to prove frothing. Then dispense a couple of drops of the mixture into each bottle using an eyedropper. A modification is simply to flick *two grains* of granulated dried yeast into each bottle. Starting with a really clear beer and dosing in a minute quantity of fresh yeast improves the quality out of proportion to the extra few minutes effort required. The matured drink will have the merest coating of yeast on the bottle bottom, permitting all but the last 2 cm. to be poured off without clouding.

Heading Liquid

Again, using the eyedropper, add *one* drop to each pint of beer.

Sweetness

Add one drop of Sweetex liquid for brown ales and two drops for sweet stouts in lieu of contrary instructions in the recipe.

Bitterness

Dilute 1 teaspoon of isomerised hop extract with 4 teaspoons of water. One drop per pint gives an extra edge of bitterness, two drops a noticeable increase.

Hop Flavour

Dilute a few drops of Hop Oil Essence in half an egg cup full of water. Dispense one drop per bottle.

Filling

After priming the bottles line them up on the floor with the bulk of beer on an adjacent table or work top.

It pays to invest in a good

syphon to make the job easier. Useful accessories at this stage are a drip tray to stand the bottle being filled on and a teacloth to mop up any spillage that could, and usually does, occur. An empty beer glass for crafty "sippers" is my personal perk as well.

Start syphoning into the first bottle with the delivery end near to the bottom to minimise fobbing. Do not fill to the brim but leave $\frac{3}{4}$ inch airspace per pint (40 mm./litre). The airspace acts as a safety reservoir to absorb conditioning gas generated in maturation.

After filling, the stopper should be loosely placed in position whilst the syphon tube is transferred to the next bottle for filling. Maintain this sequence until all the bottles are filled.

Screw stoppers and plastic reseals should be fixed as applicable and the bottles shaken to dissolve the sugar. Wipe the outside clean of spilt beer.

Crown Caps must be applied using one of the special applicator tools.

Labelling

Beer bottles look alike and some form of identification is essential where the store room contains different brews. A whole range of attractive labels are available for all styles of home brewed beer. Full size ones, blanked, so that you can write on the details yourself, are popular as well.

Crown Caps are coloured red, green, blue, brown, silver and gold and these may be used to identify different brews. Another simple means of labelling is by applying small self adhesive labels. A range of colours gives the same advantages as the crown caps. The date or other data can be written on for quick reference. Full details of the brews are best logged in a Recipe Book.

Storing

Bottles must be stored upright preferably in a dark place. The temperature of the "cellar" has usually got to fit in with your arrangements. Ideally the brew batch should be kept reasonably warm (16–20°C.) for the first week or so and then cooled to around 10–15°C.

During the first period try to monitor the progress of the secondary fermentation. The yeast sometimes adheres to the side of the bottles despite the bulk falling to form a deposit. Sharp twists daily dislodges the yeast so the brew can fall bright. An accurate impression of the clearing process is easily gained by holding a bottle up to the light.

Maturation

Naturally conditioned bottled beers need time to develop. Secondary fermentation produces the CO_2 gas for carbonation. Once this gas is formed the yeast can settle out and restore clarity; the extra pressure assists the clearing process, which should result in a more brilliant brew than before bottling.

An important physical change takes place between the liquid beer and the carbon dioxide gas. The degree which the gas dissolves affects the performance of the poured drink. Initially the gas bubbles will be large and the beer will pour like lemonade, forming a large frothy head that disappears within seconds. A nice fine creamy head results from a fine bead of bubbles and this is only achieved with time. The longer the brew is stored, the better the gas becomes dissolved, and the finer the bead will be. Clarity, condition and head retention all improve with age. The limiting factors on performance may be due to too much head being formed with old beers.

Some people query how long home brewed beer will keep. Much depends on the yeast sediment and its reaction with the beer. A good yeast will actually improve the flavour and will remain sound for years. In the majority of home brewed beer the yeast normally reaches its peak in three or four months and then starts to deteriorate. However there can be no fixed ruling on this matter and it pays to sample your beer at intervals to assess improvement or deterioration. Home brewed beer rarely goes "off" in storage. Usually the flavour becomes unpalatable with old age.

Strong beers and lagers generally benefit from a longer maturation than weak, sweet and dark beers. In all recipes, I list when my brew was first ready for sampling. Not all managed to survive to their ultimate peak of quality with maturation—they got drunk instead!

Applying crown caps with a crimping tool.

CHAPTER 6

PRESSURE BARRELS
AND DRAUGHT BEER SYSTEMS

There is a whole host of pressure barrels and CO_2 injector systems to satisfy the home brewer's love for draught beer. Keg and real ale styles of beer can be brewed at home with ease and the arrangement saves the effort of bottling.

The popular range of beer containers and carbonating aids are featured to help you make a wise choice when selecting one for your own brewing set up.

Although these highly sophisticated systems are now well tested and designed for simple operation, many users still experience problems with them. Understanding some of the mechanics and principles of operation will help to achieve better results.

Types of Barrel

There are many barrels to choose from. The types described below have special features in their design and warrant some explanation. The short history of pressure barrels for home brewing has seen many changes. Although the specification for our needs is in essence very simple, the actual practicalities of producing a reliable barrel, not prone to leaks, non toxic and possessing strength to hold relatively low gas pressures has proved to be quite difficult. New concepts, new ideas and improved models now overcome these early difficulties and the latest generation of pressure barrels have proven reliability. Home brewers are so sensitive over the service operation that no manufacturer could ever contemplate marketing a barrel now without thoroughly testing it first. Certainly this is now true from my experience and the ones described below have proved to be acceptably trouble free.

Conventional Style Barrel

The traditional barrel shape is about the only thing in common with its numerous home brew predecessors. Completely redesigned, it is now a substantial product that really does work well. Some nice features can include a threaded tap insert of hard acetal plastic embedded in the wall of the barrel which is tougher than the barrel and its tap. Thus if accidental cross threading occurs when screwing in the tap, only the tap is damaged and requires replacement. Previously the whole barrel could be ruined by such an accident. The insert, however, does not appreciate continuous contact with sterilising liquids, so do not leave such solutions in the barrel when it is empty of beer.

The range of sizes has much to recommend it. Barrel sizes available are 10, 15, 20, 25 and 50 litre. The 10 and 20 sizes have an attractive wooden grain effect on the barrel staves. And along with the white translucent 15 litre smooth ribbed version, these small sizes are ideal for small brews and for splitting large ones. Quite often I want to bottle some of a 5 gallon brew and these smaller barrels make it convenient to do so. The lifting handle has been elongated to give handling clearance to any gas injector unit fitted on to the cap.

The large 11 gallon (50 litre) barrel is really worth considering. There is not much more effort required for brewing 1, 2, 5 or 11 gallons of home brew. Producing 10 gallons in one go, gets your priorities right between drinking and brewing!

Saffron Superkeg

A 5 gallon traditional barrel with a particularly wide neck on the filler cap which permits hand access for cleaning the inside of the barrel after use. Also, because you can get your hand inside, the draw off tap is fitted with a back nut and effectively gets over the thread stripping problem discussed above.

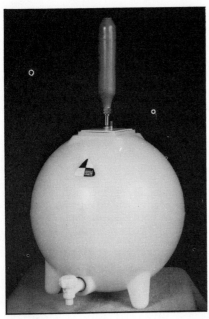

Hambleton Beersphere

The first major rethink on the pressure barrel system was the ball shaped Beersphere. Despite its "space age" look it is technically a good barrel. The 6 gallon capacity takes a normal 5 gallon brew leaving a large conditioning space above. Such an area accommodates an extra store of *natural* carbon dioxide gas to carbonate and dispense the beer without placing so much reliance on injector units.

Other desirable features are a wide neck facilitating cleaning inside as well as a drum tap with an internal locking nut.

Rotokeg

A very popular barrel incorporating many desirable features. A high level tap allows beer to be drawn off from its free standing position. A lever action float selects the clearest beer from the barrel and minimises sediment problems. Ample capacity of 6.2 gallons leaves plenty of room for storing natural CO_2 for future dispensing and carbonating of the brew. The CO_2 injector system works on the transmission valve principle. Standard 8 gm. gas bulbs and 145 and 240 gm. cylinders are available and simply screw into

the keg valve for fingertip control of gas transfer.

Other barrels can be fitted with the float system although the narrow neck types require a bit of manipulation.

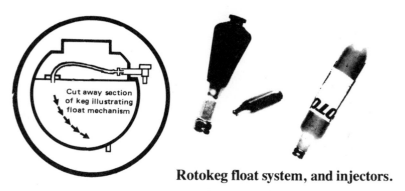

Rotokeg float system, and injectors.

Polypins are versatile storage containers for alcoholic drinks such as draught wine, sherry and now beer. Basically, they are cube shaped, flexible polythene boxes fitted with an integral filler cap and dispensing tap. Usually the Polypin or 'Ex-Wine Polythene Cube' is supported in a stout cardboard box. Common sizes are 10, 12 and 25 litre and can be purchased new from your home brew shop or secondhand at Off Licenses and Supermarkets.

The popularity of 'real ale' has seen an upsurge in their use for selling commercial draught beers over the counter. Traditional draught beer is unpressurised and ideally suits these polypins. As they do not incorporate a safety vent we must only use them for low gas content brews as well.

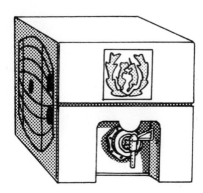

Polypin

In some of my polypins I have installed transmission valves from gas injector systems so that they can be artificially charged if the brew warrants it.

Polypins play a useful role throughout the brewing process providing a versatile container for holding racked or maturing beer besides its normal role as a cask for dispensing real ale brews.

"Drafty Five"

A 5 gallon polypin custom built for home brewers and incorporates a safety valve to ensure that the cube is not inadvertently over pressurised.

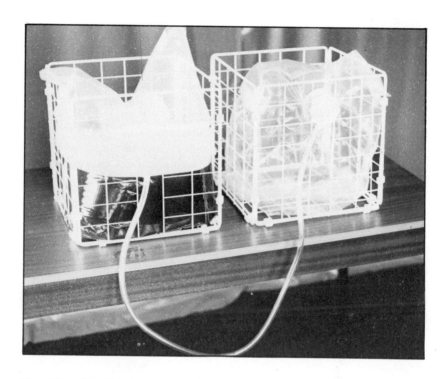

The "Bag Boy" Brewer

There are two identical units in this system for fermenting, dispensing and collecting carbon dioxide gas. Each one is comprised of a 5 gallon capacity plastic bag and filler cap cum tap and is contained in a collapsible cage.

The principle is that the brew is fermented in the first bag with its tap uppermost, and the interconnecting tubing joined on to the top of the empty second bag. The carbon dioxide liberated from the fermenting beer is transferred to the other and stored. Any excess gas is vented by the safety valve band around the filler cap neck.

At the end of fermentation, the beer bag is squeezed to discharge the brew to the second "gas" bag where the stored carbon dioxide conditions it.

The beer has then been fermented and conditioned without danger and spoilage from air and is covered at all times by a protective blanket of CO_2. When dispensing, the gas is trapped above the beer and the bag collapses as the beer is drawn off.

Cornelius Beer Pressure System

A complete professional system for the homebrewer. Make your own pub bar with this arrangement! Basically the brew is contained in a 5 U.S. gallon (approximately 4 imperial gallons) stainless steel cylinder. Natural CO_2 given off by the fermenting brew is retained in the cylinder. The relief valve lifts around 135 p.s.i. so a tremendous amount of gas can be stored and used later to dispense the beer. A gas bottle, pressure gauges, regulator, bar tap and drip tray complete this impressive system. Although relatively expensive, this trouble free system is good value and has much to offer.

Gas Injector Systems

CO_2 gas injector systems are recommended with all pressure barrels to back up the natural supply of carbon dioxide given off from the beer inside. As beer is drawn off, the pressure is used up ejecting the brew in a lively state. The more beer consumed, the "flatter" it becomes as the conditioning gas liberates to fill the space left by the drawn off pints. Once the gas has been used up the only way to get the beer out of the barrel is to allow air to bubble back through the tap. Air in contact with beer can deteriorate the flavour to the point of being unpalatable within a day and risks contamination if left any longer.

A burst of CO_2 gas restores condition as well as maintaining a protective sterile environment. There are some novel ways of achieving this.

Basic Filler Cap Mounted Injector

Designed to fit on to the filler caps of the conventional barrel shaped barrels. The unit comprises a T-shaped injector body which houses the control valve for regulating the supply of gas from the cartridge bulb. Each bulb contains carbon dioxide gas pressurised to the liquid state. The bulb holder can usually accommodate both the standard 8 gm. bulb or the larger 12 gm. size. Incorporated in the control valve, which protrudes from the opposite end from the bulb, is a rubber sleeve and this acts as a safety valve for limiting the pressure in the barrel to the maximum working pressure of 10 p.s.i.

When buying one of these injectors it pays to get a new filler cap with a hole in it ready to accept the units, (if not already fitted, as they usually are nowadays). There is a large bolt on the underside of the injector body. Take it off and pass it back through the filler cap hole into the injector again. Tighten hand tight only and replace the combined unit on the barrel and screw on the filler cap firmly. In this position *gently* rotate the injector so that it sits at right angles to the axis of the handle. Now that the injector unit has been lined up so that it will not foul the handle in the service position, it can be finally clamped together. This must be done with extreme caution as *stripped threads are not normally covered by the guarantee*. The metal nut can ruin the plastic thread in the injector body so easily with over zealous action on the spanner. About half a turn from the hand tight position should be enough.

Using It

1. Before actually putting a cartridge in the injector, I like to prepare all the bulbs by wiping the merest smear of petroleum jelly around the neck of each one. The extra lubrication makes retrieval of the spent bulbs easier and minimises the risk of damage to the "O" ring seals in the injector body.

2. The gas injector should be loaded and checked before putting on the barrel. Remove the bulb holder, drop in a gas cartridge and *loosely* screw back on to the injector. Check that the control valve at the other end is closed before the bulb holder is screwed in further to puncture the cartridge. A short sharp hiss should be heard whilst screwing in. No further audible escape of gas should be detected providing an effective seal has been made. The injector is ready for service.

3. Syphon or fill the barrel with beer as normal leaving a few pints of ullage space.

4. Screw the injector unit on to the barrel. Gently crack open the control valve to hear a continuous hiss from the gas being transferred to the barrel. Close the valve when the safety valve rubber lifts to vent the extra build up of gas.

5. The brew is still best left for the priming sugar to condition it for a week or so.

6. Draw off the beer as required. When the pressure falls, open the control valve and let more gas into the barrel.

7. When replacing spent bulbs, remember to check that the control valve is closed first.

Pressure Gauge

A pressure gauge mounted on the filler cap will give a direct indication of the CO_2 pressure in the barrel. It serves many useful purposes regards safety and operating efficiency.

A cheap and popular pressure gauge.

The maximum working pressure is stamped on all pressure barrels and ranges from 10 lb. per square inch (10 p.s.i.) to 25 p.s.i. These barrels are usually supplied with a plain filler cap and may be used as a "bunged cask" where the build up of gas cannot be vented, and a pressure gauge is the only safe way of telling when the conditions inside are becoming too dangerous for comfort.

Gas Injector Systems rely on the safety valves to limit the pressure to a reasonable level and a pressure gauge can be used to prove these are functioning correctly.

A suitable scale range is from 0–30 p.s.i., and the beer should be kept between 2–7 p.s.i. when possible for balanced carbonation.

Hambleton Bard Injectors

Two types of injector are available for the Beersphere. The standard type uses the normal 8 gm. Sparklet bulbs and the De-Luxe model uses the Hambleton S20 Carbon dioxide cylinder.

The injector unit is in two parts. A transmission valve fits on to the underside filler hole plate as a permanent feature. This allows gas into the Beersphere and keeps it in. To get the gas in, a detachable

bulb holder, the other half of the injector system, screws on to the transmission valve thread where it seals and then opens another valve in the holder to release gas from the cartridge bulb. To stop the flow simply unscrew again.

One bulb holder will service a number of barrels so long as they are fitted with transmission valves. These are relatively cheap and can be purchased separately.

De-Luxe S20 and S30 Injector System

The S30 cylinder is the most economical system in the long term as the cost of gas is less than half of that of the standard 8 gm. bulb. One integral transmission valve and safety vest sits on the barrel and the giant 20 gm. cylinder screws in to inject its contents. This arrangement is proving a winner for its consistent reliable performance.

As with the standard injector this one may be fitted on to the caps of most types of plastic pressure barrels.

Grapehop Injector

A real giant injector based on the Sodastream 8 oz. CO_2 gas cylinder that has the capacity of thirty standard bulbs!

One injector fitted to the cylinder will service any number of barrels fitted with the appropriate transmission valve. The feature I like is the inherent safety of the injector. To get gas to flow, the injector is simply pushed on to the transmission valve where it seals; further pressure opens the control valve.

Because there is no mechanical coupling the gas cylinder cannot be inadvertently exhausted into the barrel.

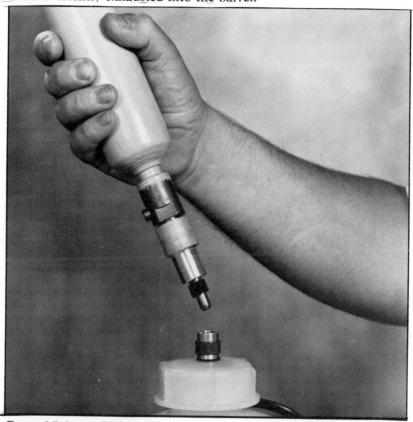

Care of Injector Units

The Gas Injector Units are precision machined and moulded to cope safely with the very high pressures found in the cartridge bulbs. Beer, being a slightly acidic liquid, is mildly corrosive to metal. Any metal parts exposed in direct contact or subjected to the humid carbon dioxide atmosphere above the beer will suffer.

After the barrel has been emptied of beer, remove the filler cap and injector and wash thoroughly under cold running water. Never use sterilising solution for prolonged contact with injectors as this aggravates corrosion. The large nut on the underside is particularly prone to this trouble. Always inspect it to see if the bore is clear as a blockage here could cause a nasty accident. The nut must be removed to facilitate clearing of any bubbles of corrosion. Buy a new nut if there is any doubt on its condition. Check the physical condition of the rubber washers, safety valve sleeve and the state of the plastic body. The main items rarely need any attention, but if necessary new parts can be bought.

Normally the only wearable parts are the 'O' ring seals and these can be replaced quite easily by a mechanically minded person. The safest approach is to return the unit via your local home brew shop to the manufacturer who has the facilities to test and service properly.

Blow Bag

A novel system relying on 'puff power' from your mouth to replace the role of the CO_2 cartridge bulb for dispensing your beer. Other systems call for a burst of CO_2 from the injector system to produce pressure to dispense the beer and creates a sterile environment to keep it free from contamination. Injecting the full contents of a barrel often uses up to four or five bulbs and it is an expensive item on the brewing budget.

When pressure falls in the barrel fitted with a blow bag, you simply inflate the balloon to restore the balance.

CO_2 Collector

The Blow Bag does not provide CO_2 gas and hence cannot carbonate the brew. Normal priming can be followed or alternatively *free* CO_2 gas can be collected from the copious supplies given off by beer in the fermenting bin. This gas is sucked off and stored in a special canister. A tube adaptor fits on to the barrel tap and the gas from the Collector Kit is squeezed in. By recycling and recharging a clear beer can be carbonated and conditioned without resorting to priming. Any size flexible canister or plastic bag can be used as a collector.

CHAPTER 7

RECIPES

After introducing the brewing ingredients and discussing the options on equipment and procedures in some detail, the information is condensed and presented as a full range of exciting recipes for bitters, lagers, stouts and other beers for you to try.

The chapter on recipes is the most important section of the book for the author and reader alike. All the previous explanations of brewing ingredients and procedures are designed to give the reader no more than an appreciation of the process on the first reading. My instructions in the recipes inevitably must be a short precis of the whole procedure. Indeed, it cannot be, nor is it intended to be, any more than a guideline for brewing that beer. So much of the success depends on the quality of the ingredients, the brewing method and the equipment you use, that each recipe must be assessed on how you are actually going to brew it.

Most of the recipe instructions are based on the minimum requirements to produce a reasonable beer. I reiterate my earlier quote that success hinges on "Quality versus Convenience". The more effort you put into selecting ingredients, storing them correctly and implementing the extra tasks for quality control on the process side, the better the beer will be.

For example, let us consider the Trafalgar Bitter recipe as regards hops. You could satisfy the recipe requirements and use the remaining 4 oz. of Goldings from the 1 lb. bag purchased last year. If they have been kept at normal room temperature for months the chances of imparting a fresh hop flavour to the brew are negligible. The bitterness would be under par as well. However, if the hop sample has been stored in the deep freezer or refrigerator, the hops would still be as fresh as the day they were bought.

Maybe your home brew stockist only has Golding Hop Pellets. Could you use these? Well yes, of course, and by referring back to my comments you will see that they can be thoroughly recommended. Probably only 2 oz. of pellets are needed to replace 4 oz. of fresh hops depending on their concentration. The recipe instructions ask for the hops to be boiled for 45 minutes. In discussion of wort boiling I show that it can be advantageous not to put in all the hops at once. Dosing in proportions throughout the boil improves the hop flavour. Even saving a small handful for "dry hopping" in the barrel is a sound practice.

The other options include using hop extract, isomerised hop extracts which demand a different approach. Just by picking on one ingredient, shows the enormous choice open to using that ingredient. A choice that you must make. The trouble is that it all tends to become confusing until you can develop an understanding of these topics and some brewers prefer the convenience of simplicity and no doubt they will "boil 4 oz. of Goldings for 45 minutes" as instructed—without any variation!

Recipe Information Explained

Each recipe will only give the basic facts about the brewing ingredients and method. The main list of ingredients is flanked by both imperial and metric quantities. Do not, however, cross reference the two systems as the final volumes of beer will not be the same, i.e. 5 gallons is not equivalent to 25 litres and the ingredients list reflects this difference. In some instances where a product is conveniently available only in one weight system (e.g. 1 kg. bag of sugar) then it may be found on both sides if its influence on the balance of the beer can be ignored.

Minor ingredients and brewing aids such as Irish Moss, yeast nutrient and finings may be commented on together with other relevant snippets of information before actually tackling the main method instructions.

116

TRAFALGAR BITTER

An easy to brew bitter with the power to blow your head off!

5 gallons	Original Gravity 1047/50	25 litres
4 lb.	Malt extract	2 kg.
8 oz.	Crushed crystal malt	250 gm.
4 oz.	Goldings hops	125 gm.
2 lb.	White sugar	1 kg.
1 lb.	Soft brown sugar	500 gm.
	Dried beer yeast	

The malt extract can be the standard liquid (medium grade) or the light dried variety and must be boiled in the minimum of $2\frac{1}{2}$ gallons (12 litres) of water. Proprietary pale ale/bitter water treatment salts should be added if necessary. Using dried extract will raise the starting gravity to 1050. In place of the Goldings hops I have used Hallertau and Fuggles with equal success. Other aids I would recommend are Irish Moss, yeast nutrient with or without header and beer finings. When priming the rate will be $\frac{1}{2}$ teaspoon/pint or 2–3 oz. per barrel.

Method:

1. Boil the malt extract and hops in water for 45 minutes. Meanwhile:

2. Make up a yeast starter.

3. Dissolve the sugar in boiling water, cool awhile and pour into a sterilised fermenting bin.

4. Place the crystal malt in a saucepan, cover well with boiling water and simmer for a few minutes. Strain off the liquor into the bin. Repeat process to extract more goodness.

Then:

5. Strain off the hopped wort as well and top up the bin with cold water to the final volume.

6. When cool to room temperature, pitch in the yeast and ferment the brew until the gravity falls to 1008.

7. Rack off the beer and keep under airlock protection.

8. When reasonably clear, bottle or cask as required remembering to prime each vessel appropriately. ($\frac{1}{2}$ teaspoon/pint or $\frac{1}{2}$ oz./ gallon.)

9. Sample the draught brew after one week and the bottled version in two weeks.

117

MARLBOROUGH MILD ALE
From brewing to burping! this tasty mild is ready in 10 days.

5 gallons	Original Gravity 1035	25 litres
3 lb.	Dark malt extract	1½ kg.
2 lb.	Brown sugar	1 kg.
1 oz.	Northdown hop pellets	30 gm.
5	Saccharin tablets	5
	Dried beer yeast	

Use dried dark extract, S.F.X. or Muntona Dark Grade or similar and boil in a minimum of 2 gallons (10 litres) of water to which proprietary Mild Ale crystals have been added as necessary. The saccharins are optional, but I would advise you to use them to demonstrate how they can smooth out harshness in a young beer.

Method:
1. Boil the malt extract and pellets in water for 30 minutes.
Meanwhile:
2. Make up a yeast starter.
3. Dissolve the brown sugar in boiling water, cool awhile and pour into a sterilised fermenting bin.

Then:
Switch off the boiler and let the hopped wort settle. Pour or strain off as much clear liquid as possible. Add some of the cold topping up water to the hop debris in the boiler. Stir and allow to settle again. Another straining off should retrieve the majority of valuable extract caught up with the redundant pellets. A small amount of hop substances carried over to the bin is acceptable and can be strained off with the initial yeast crop. Too much, however will affect fermentation.

Adjust the volume to the final gallonage. Pitch with the yeast starter when cool and ferment down to 1006. Rack and allow to stand for a day or so under airlocks before casking in a barrel or polypin. Prime with 3 oz. or 2 oz. respectively as appropriate. Try the brew three days later.

BULLDOG BROWN ALE

Based on an old fashioned tasty commercial brew.

5 gallons	Original Gravity 1036	25 litres
4 lb.	Dark malt extract	2 kg.
4 oz.	Crushed crystal malt	125 gm.
1½ oz.	Crushed black malt	45 gm.
1 oz.	Northern brewer hops	30 gm.
1½ oz.	Fuggles or Northdown hops	45 gm.
1 lb.	Brown sugar	500 gm.
3 oz.	Lactose	100 gm.
	Dried beer or stout yeast	

Good quality Lactose imparts a smooth sweetness to the malt body. Beware of "cheesy" smelling samples. A recipe like this is worth trying to assess the flavour of Lactose compared with the more convenient artificial sweeteners. One drop of Sweetex liquid (or equivalent) per pint is the alternative dosing. Heading liquid is strongly recommended when bottling. Use at the same rate as the Sweetex liquid.

Method:

1. Boil the malt extract and hops for 45 minutes, but save about one third of the quota of Northern Brewer to near the end of the boil... meanwhile ...
2. Make up the yeast starter.
3. Dissolve the brown sugar in boiling water, switch off and stir in the Lactose. Cool awhile and pour into the sterilised bin.
4. Place the crystal and black malt in a saucepan, cover with boiling water and simmer for a few minutes. Strain of the liquor into the bin. Repeat the process to extract more goodness.

Then:

5. Strain off the hopped wort and top up the bin with cold water to the final volume.
6. When cool to room temperature pitch in the yeast starter and ferment the brew under a loosely covered lid until the gravity is below 1006.
7. Rack off the beer and keep under airlock protection for a few days.
8. When reasonably clear, syphon into bottles which have been primed with sugar and heading liquid.
9. Mature two weeks before drinking.

FULL BODIED STOUTS

A suite of remarkably good stouts. If stout is your tipple, then these recipes are a must.

BELFAST BREW

A dry stout.

5 gallons	Original Gravity 1045	25 litres
5 lb.	Malt extract syrup	2½ kg.
1 lb.	Roast barley (whole)	500 gm.
2.2 lb.	White sugar	1 kg.
4 oz.	Hops	125 gm.
	Dried stout yeast	

Do not use a caramel coloured dark malt syrup. Medium, Amber or D.M.S. grades are best for this dry stout. Another departure from my earlier recommendations is the use of *whole* barley grains. For some reason whole grains have proved to be smoother than when I experimented with a smaller measure of crushed grains. The hops choice has been left open as I was pleased with the following variations and reckoned that other changes would prove satisfactory as well.

1st Choice: ½ oz. Bullion (15 gm.)
3½ oz. Fuggles (110 gm.)

2nd Choice: 1 oz. Northern Brewer (30 gm.)
3 oz. Northdown (100 gm.)

I found the use of the yeast nutrient and heading salts particularly good here. I wanted some artificial heading but not too much as could be dosed in with the liquid variety. Cultivating a yeast starter from a bottle of Guinness would be a step in the right direction as well.

YEOMAN STOUT

The sweet version.

5 gallons	Original Gravity 1045	25 litres
5 lb.	Dark or S.F.X. malt extract	2½ kg.
1 lb.	Chocolate malt (whole)	500 gm.
2.2 lb.	White sugar	1 kg.
3 oz.	Mixed hops	100 gm.
	Beer or Stout yeast	
	Saccharin or similar	

120

Again the roast grain must be used whole. Although I have not tried it, black malt could be substituted for the chocolate variety. The additional richness of the patent black may need reducing by cutting down on the quantity used.

Method:
1. Boil the malt extract and malt grains for 45 minutes. Meanwhile:
2. Make up yeast starter.
3. Dissolve the sugar in boiling water, cool awhile and pour into a sterilised fermenting bin.
4. Strain off the hopped wort into sterilised fermenting bin and top up with cold water to the final volume.
5. When cool to room temperature, pitch in the yeast and ferment the brew until the gravity falls to 1008.
6. Rack off the beer and keep under airlock protection.
7. When reasonably clear, bottle or cask the brew as required. Remember to dose the Yeoman Stout with artificial sweetener to achieve the right degree of sweetness.
8. Sample after two weeks.

DIPLOMAT STRONG LAGER

4 gallons	Original Gravity 1048	20 litres
4 lb.	National or light malt extract syrup	2 kg.
2 lb.	Glucose chips	1 kg.
3 oz.	Hallertau hops	100 gm.
	Dried lager yeast	

Method:
Base on "Trafalgar Bitter" recipe.

ANCHOR ALE

A hoppy Pale Ale.

5 gallons	Original Gravity 1038	25 litres
4 lb.	D.M.S. or medium malt extract	2 kg.
1 lb.	Glucose chips	500 gm.
1 lb.	Soft brown sugar	500 gm.
2 oz.	Northdown hops	60 gm.
1 oz.	Goldings hops	30 gm.
	British Ale yeast	

Method:
Base on "Trafalgar Bitter" recipe.

MARQUIS BARLEY WINE

1 gallon	Original Gravity 1090	4.55 litres
2 lb.	Muntona light malt extract or Edme D.M.S.	1.8 kg.
1 lb.	Invert sugar	350 gm.
1½ oz.	Best Goldings hops	45 gm.
1 teaspoon per pint	Cream sherry	10 ml./litre
	C.W.E. wine yeast or similar	

Method:

1. Boil the malt extract, invert sugar and hops in just over 1 gallon (5 litres) of water for 45 minutes.
2. Allow to cool and then strain off into a gallon jar.
3. Add yeast and ferment under airlock for about 10 days in a warm place. Rack off the brew from the heavy sediment into another gallon jar. Top up to the base of the neck with cooled boiled water. Replace airlock and leave until ferment ends at around S.G. 1010–15.
4. Syphon off into bottles (preferably "nips") which have been primed with cream sherry.
5. Mature the Marquis for at least six months before drinking.

A selection of recipes using.
BOOTS MALT EXTRACT
All the ingredients used are normally available in the larger retail outlets with a home brew section.

NOTTINGHAM PALE ALE (40 pints)
4 lb. tin of Boots malt extract
1 kg. white sugar
4 oz. Goldings hops
Sachet of brewing yeast

Nottingham Pale Ale is a basic bitter brew. The white sugar may be replaced with the soft dark brown variety for a change.

SPARTAN BITTER (40 pints)
2 lb. Boots malt extract
2 lb. Demerara sugar
5 Boots saccharin tablets
3 oz. Fuggles hops
Sachet of brewing yeast

A light bitter, smooth and ready to drink within a couple of weeks.

BRITANNIA BITTER (40 pints)
4 lb. Boots malt extract
4 oz. crushed crystal malt
1 lb. white sugar
1 lb. golden syrup
1 tub Inn Sign hop extract
Sachet of brewing yeast

A high class bitter. The hop extract could be replaced by 4 oz. of loose hops or equivalent weight of hop pellets. Goldings or Hallertau are the best choices here.

BUCKINGHAM BROWN ALE (40 pints)
2 lb. Boots malt extract
$\frac{1}{4}$ lb. crushed crystal malt
4 teaspoon Brewers caramel
8 Boots saccharin tablets
1 sachet of brewing yeast
2 lb. brown sugar

A nice light brown ale. If you prefer a darker, more malty brew, then simply throw in a small handful of whole black malt grains when boiling the extract and hops. Both versions can be drawn from the barrel as a draught mild ale.

FINE LIGHT ALE (32 pints)
2 lb. Boots malt extract
1 lb. light brown sugar
2 oz. Hallertau hops
1 sachet of brewing yeast

SAMSON STOUT (24 pints)

2 lb. Boots malt extract
½ lb. whole black malt grains
¼ lb. whole crystal malt
1 tub of Inn Sign hop extract
(12 Boots saccharin tablets, optional to produce a sweet stout)
1 sachet of brewing yeast   1 kg. white sugar

When collecting the ingredients from the recipe list remember to purchase any water treatment salts as required, i.e. Pale Ale salts for Bitters, Pale and Lights and Mild Ale for the dark brews. Other useful aids are yeast nutrient, gelatine beer finings and Campden tablets.

Method for all recipes:

1. Boil the malt extract with all the quota of malt grains, hops and hop extract in sufficient water for 30-45 minutes.
   Meanwhile:
2. Remove a little boiling wort, dilute with cold water to cool to room temperature and sprinkle in a sachet of yeast to make a yeast starter.
3. Dissolve the sugar or syrup in boiling water, cool awhile and pour into a sterilised fermenting bin.
4. Strain the hopped wort into the bin and discard the solid debris. Top up to the final volume with cold water.
5. When cool to room temperature pitch in the yeast starter mixture, a small spoonful of yeast nutrient and the Gelatine finings. Replace the lid on loosely and ferment the brew in a warm place until the specific gravity falls to around 1006. Rouse the brew twice daily to assist fermentation.
6. When the beer has finished working, clean off any surface scum, add *two* crushed Campden tablets and snap the fermenting bin lid on tight. Leave undisturbed for two days.
7. Bottle the brew, priming each bottle with ½ teaspoon of white sugar per pint of capacity;
   or
   Cask the brew in a pressure barrel priming each gallon with ½ oz. of sugar.
8. Start sampling after a weeks maturation.

BARLEY SYRUP RECIPES

The next brew invite the use of Barley Syrup; a much underrated malt syrup. The lighter and more delicate flavour overcomes the strong maltiness found with some malt extracts.

BARLEY MOW BITTER

5 gallons	Original Gravity 1038	25 litres
2 lb.	Malt extract	1 kg.
2 lb.	Barley syrup	1 kg.
2 lb.	Golden syrup	1 kg.
4 oz.	Goldings hops	125 gm.
	Dried beer yeast	

Use Pale Ale/Bitter water treatment as appropriate. Irish Moss in the boil, yeast nutrient for fermentation and Beer finings are recommended aids as well. Challenger hops are a fuller flavoured substitute for Goldings.

MALTHOUSE MILD

5 gallons	Original Gravity 1036	25 litres
2 lb.	Dark malt extract	1 kg.
2 lb.	Barley syrup	1 kg.
1½ lb.	Soft brown sugar	750 gm.
2 oz.	Crushed black malt	60 gm.
2 oz.	Northdown hops	60 gm.
10	Saccharin tablets	10
	Dried stout yeast	

Mild ales have a low hop rate and any of the common varieties would work here as substitutes. Fermenting with proper wet brewery yeast would eliminate the call for saccharin tablets.

VICEROY LAGER

5 gallons	Original Gravity 1043	25 litres
1 kg.	Muntona light malt extract	1 kg.
2 lb.	Barley syrup	1 kg.
1 kg.	White sugar	1 kg.
2 oz.	Hallertau hops	60 gm.
	Dried lager yeast	

An easy brew with a true continental flavour. Standard brewing aids of Irish Moss, yeast nutrient and heading agent are advised here.

The common brewing method is the straightforward malt extract technique as is demonstrated in the "Trafalgar Bitter" recipe.

MORE HOPPED WORT RECIPES

These are just a few recipes from what has proved to be a very versatile technique for home brewing.

IMPERIAL PALE ALE

5 gallons	Imperial Pale Ale	25 litres
1	Cordon Brew Export Pale Ale hopped wort (36 pint size)	1
1 oz.	Hallertau hops	30 gm.
1 lb.	Light dried malt extract	500 gm.
2 lb.	White sugar	1 kg.
	Yeast provided	

Method:
1. Dissolve the malt extract in sufficient hot water. Add hops and boil for 10 minutes.

Meanwhile:
2. Dissolve the sugar in boiling water, cool awhile and pour into a sterilised fermenting bin.
3. Empty in can of hopped wort and rinse out with two "canfuls" of hot water.

Then:
4. Strain the boiled wort into the fermenting bin. Top up with cold water, cover and allow to cool to room temperature.
5. Sprinkle in the yeast provided and ferment the brew in a warm place.
6. When fermentation abates, skim off any surface scum and stir in two crushed Campden tablets. Snap the fermenting bin lid on tight and leave for two days undisturbed.
7. Syphon into primed beer bottles or pressure barrel and leave two weeks before drinking.

TALBOT BITTER

5 gallons		25 litre
2 lb.	Edme pale ale wort	914 gm.
2 lb.	Edme D.M.S.	914 gm.
1 lb.	Glucose Chips	500 gm.
1 oz.	Golding hops	30 gm.
1 oz.	Northern brewer hops	30 gm.
	Yeast provided	

Method:
As per "Imperial Pale Ale" recipe.

SILVER STAR LAGER

5 gallons		25 litre
3.3 lb.	Muntona lager wort	1½ kg.
1 oz.	Crushed crystal malt	30 gm.
1 teaspoon (heaped)	Hallertau hop pellets	10 ml.
2 lb.	White sugar	1 kg.
	Lager yeast	

Method:
The crushed crystal malt replaces the malt extract in the boiling instructions. Otherwise method the same as for "Imperial Pale Ale"..

STAG STRONG ALE

5 gallons		25 litre
2 lb.	Edme bitter wort	914 gm.
2 lb.	Edme barley wort wine	914 gm.
1 lb.	Glucose chips	500 gm.
2 lb.	Demerara sugar	1 kg.
	Yeast provided	

Method:
Similar procedure to "Imperial Pale Ale" recipe omitting stage 1 and part of stage 4 which refers to boiling of certain ingredients.

Recipes That Should Not Work But Do!

The scope and variety of recipes for standard malt extract brewing is rather limited and should exclude all the starch based grains such as pale malt, wheat, rice, maize and a whole host of other cereals in widespread use in commercial brewing. That is, until now!

Normally any other cereal must be "mashed" to convert its starchy interior into sugar before it becomes compatible in the home brewing chain. However, during mashing experiments some test went wrong and much of the starch was left unconverted. Rather than waste it, the brew was made up and found to be very good. A nice grainy taste to the beer was achieved, but with no starch haze marring clarity. Further tests proved it was possible to use flaked maize, rice, barley, wheat malt and many other grains with almost as much versatility as a "grain" recipe.

Do not allow these adjuncts to be boiled for more than three minutes if mashing has been bypassed

Pale malt grains	*used for*	True beer flavour
Mild ale malt grains	„	Grain taste and colour
Lager malt grain	„	Lager flavour
Flaked barley	„	Head retention
Flaked rice	„	Reduces malt extract "tang"
Flaked maize	„	Corn flavour for lager
Wheat malt grains	„	Head retention and flavour
Wheat flour	„	Head retention
Breakfast cereals	„	Head retention and flavour

BOUNTY BITTER

5 gallons	Original Gravity 1035	25 litres
3 lb.	Dark malt extract	1½ kg.
3 oz.	Crystal malt	100 gm.
3 oz.	Crushed wheat malt	100 gm.
2 lb.	Brown sugar	1 kg.
2 oz.	Hallertau hops	60 gm.
1 oz.	Challenger hops	30 gm.
	Dried beer yeast	

Use Pale Ale/Bitter water treatment as appropriate. Employ Irish Moss in the boil, nutrient in the fermentation and heading agent when casking. The wheat malt could be replaced by one Weetabix biscuit.

Method:

1. Boil the malt extract, crystal malt and the hops for 45 minutes. *Throw in the wheat malt for the last three minutes of the boil.*

Meanwhile:

2. Make up a yeast starter.
3. Dissolve the sugar in boiling water, cool awhile and pour into a sterilised fermenting bin.

Then:

4. Strain the hopped wort into the bin and top up to the final volume with cold water.
5. Pitch in the yeast starter and ferment the brew for 4–5 days until the S.G. falls to 1006.
6. Rack into a polythene cube or gallon jars and add beer finings and heading agent.
7. Syphon into bottles or a cask and prime accordingly.

BLACK PRINCE

A smooth, dark, sweet stout.

5 gallons	Original Gravity 1040	25 litres
4 lb.	Dark malt syrup	2 kg.
5 oz.	Crushed black malt	150 gm.
4 oz.	Flaked barley	125 gm.
4 oz.	Lactose	125 gm.
2 lb.	White sugar	1 kg.
2 oz.	Northern brewer hops	60 gm.
	Dried stout yeast	

Method:

As per "Bounty Bitter", except use Mild Ale water treatment instead of Pale Ale Salts. The brew should be bottled only.

FEST PILSNER

5 gallons	Original Gravity	25 litres
3.3 lb.	Muntona light malt extract	1½ kg.
4 oz.	Crushed lager malt grains	125 gm.
2 lb.	White sugar	1 kg.
2 oz.	Seedless hops	60 gm.
	Dried lager yeast	

Method:

As per "Bounty Bitter". The hops can be Hallertau, Saaz or Styrian Goldings. My trials worked well using 1 oz. of Hallertau hop pellets.

ECONOMY BREWS

A very acceptable satisfying beer can be brewed for about a tenth of the price of commercial brews.

CHEER BEER BITTER

40 pints		25 litres
1 lb.	Crushed crystal malt	500 gm.
2 oz.	Hops	60 gm.
4 lb.	White sugar	2 kg.
	Dried beer or stout yeast	
Plus:	½ teaspoon lactic or citric acid	
	2 teaspoon yeast nutrient	
	1 teaspoon heading liquid	
	Beer finings	
40 pints	Cheer Beer Mild Ale	25 litres

As ingredients for Cheer Beer Bitter;

Plus: 2 oz.	Crushed black malt	60 gm.

Method:

1. Contain the crushed malt grains and hops in a muslin bag and boil in as much water as practicable. Strain off the liquid extract into a sterilised fermenting bin. Repeat the boiling and straining off two or three times more to extract as much goodness as possible.
2. Dissolve the sugar in boiling water, cool awhile and add to the fermenting bin as well.

3. Top up to the final volume with cold water and allow to cool to room temperature.

4. Stir in the yeast, nutrient, acid and heading liquid and allow the brew to ferment in a reasonably warm environment.

5. When fermentation comes to an end around a specific gravity of 1002, skim off surface scum, stir in the beer finings and two crushed Campden tablets (optional) and snap the lid on tight. Leave for two days undisturbed.

6. Syphon the beer into bottles or a pressure barrel as required. Prime bottles with $\frac{1}{2}$ teaspoon of white sugar per pint or $\frac{1}{2}$ oz. per gallon in the cask.

7. Mature for 10 days before supping.

Low Alcohol Beer

Brewing weak beer or a concoction that would not even rate technically as being strong enough to be called beer may seem at first against the ideals of home brewers. However, legal and social factors place restrictions on what is regarded as over indulgence in our hobby.

Restricting the intake of alcohol for car drivers is obviously a very desirable law, but nevertheless it does stifle enjoyment for beer drinkers. I just cannot tolerate standing about supping dry ginger or other non alcoholic liquids as a precaution for driving home.

Determined to do something about it, I devised two recipes brewed with malt, hops, yeast and water with virtually no alcohol in it. In fact 150 pints of Low Alcer beer contains less alcohol than an average pint of home brew!

Drivers and Slimmers Beer
Ingredients for 1 *gallon*

LOW ALCER BITTER BEER

8 oz.	**Crushed crystal malt**
3 oz.	**Burton body brew**
$\frac{1}{2}$ oz.	**Hops**
$\frac{1}{2}$ teaspoon	**Heading liquid**
1 teaspoon	**Dried yeast**

LOW ALCER BROWN ALE

8 oz.	Crushed crystal malt
½ oz.	Crushed black malt grains
3 oz.	Burton body brew
2	Saccharin tablets
½ teaspoon	Heading liquid
½ oz.	Hops
1 teaspoon	Dried yeast

Method:
1. Boil malt, hops and Burton body brew (Malto Dextrin powder) in 1 gallon of water for five minutes. Switch off and allow to cool.
2. Carefully strain off the clear liquid into a sterilised gallon jar. Top up to the base of the neck with cold water and when cool to room temperature add the yeast, heading liquid and saccharin if required.
3. Fit an airlock to the demi-john and allow the brew to rest for two days.
4. Syphon into beer bottles priming each with a scant level teaspoonful of sugar.
5. Mature in a warm place for one week and drink within a month.

Beer Kit Variations

Impart a More Grainy Taste
Simmer a broken Weetabix biscuit, or a small handful of flaked barley in boiling water for a few minutes. Cool and add the clear liquid as part of the top up water.

Sugars
Substitute part or all of the white sugar quota with brown sugars, glucose chips or powder, invert sugar, golden syrup and treacles. Go cautiously with the strong flavoured syrups.

Hops
"Dry Hop" the brew by sprinkling a few powdered hop pellets on the surface of the fermenting beer when the initial yeast crop has subsided.

CHAPTER 8

MASHING WITH
MALT EXTRACT

Nearly all Commercial breweries use cereal adjuncts to supplement the extract and flavour of the malted barley. Maize, rice and un-malted barley grain are often added because it is technically desirable to do so. Better flavour, clearer colour, firmer foam heads and longer shelf lives are achieved. Using these adjuncts gives the home brewer far more scope to brew the beer he wants, economically, and with more chance of success. To integrate these cereals into the brewing chain they must be mashed with a hot solution of diastatic malt extract to convert their starchy interiors to usuable sugar.

The advanced recipes incorporating adjuncts demonstrate the infinite range of beer styles and flavours that it is now possible to brew.

The normal malt extract brewing approach starts with the boiling process and the ingredients used are basically starch free malted grains or syrups and a range of sugars. Starch based cereals can be incorporated in our beers for economy and flavour changes, but like our commercial counterparts, we must indulge in some pre-treatment.

Mashing is the term used to describe the process for changing the added starch to useful fermentable extract. In the brewery, mashing is an essential process because the main starting ingredient, pale malt barley grains, require this treatment anyway. Just adding some more cereals to the grist is simple and makes a great deal of sense technically.

The merits in home brewing of using *adjuncts*, as these added cereals are called, needs consideration.

Malt extract syrups have already been mashed and hence to repeat the process means more work, more skill and possibly more equipment. However, there is much to savour on the credit side as better flavoured and quality brews can be achieved. There is no getting away from the fact that malt extract, possibly because of the heat treatment during the concentration process can leave a characteristic tang on the palate not found with worts from dilute mashes in commercial establishments or home brew "grain" recipes employing similar techniques. It is analogous to the grape concentrates used by winemakers. No one would really expect the concentrated juice to be reconstituted and fermented into a vintage wine. We have the same problems, and indeed if malt extract alone could rival the traditional mashed extract, then the breweries would have changed over to it lock, stock and barrel years ago!

The trend to use malt extract commercially is increasing and there are no complaints so far. It is extremely difficult to detect with any degree of certainty substitutions of malt extract up to 30 per cent.

The flavour of the better commercial brews are now within our grasp if we employ mashing techniques as well.

Ingredients for Mashing

Diastatic Malt Extract

Where adjuncts are used in the formulation and need converting to fermentable extract, only the *diastatic* type of malt syrup is suitable. Edme D.M.S. and Muntona Century are the only ones available to us. Unless otherwise stated they are completely interchangeable in recipes.

Pale Malt Grains

Commercial breweries base their beers on malted barley grains and sometimes supplement these with malt extract and other adjuncts. We tackle it from the opposite angle. Our recipes are mainly malt extract syrups and we can use these grains to produce interesting variations. As with the diastatic malt syrups, these grains have the power to convert other cereal starches to sugar. Pale Malt is the traditional brewing ingredient and is by far the best for us to use on quality considerations. It is preferable to buy the grain already crushed as the degree of milling affects its conversion ability.

Mild Ale Malt Grains

A slightly darker malt designed for milds, browns and stouts. Similar properties to the pale variety.

Amber Malt Grains

An uncommon malt in home brew shops. It is a special malt, smoke roasted to light amber colour, and has a distinctive woody aroma and flavour.

Lager Malt Grains

The continental version of our pale malt and is used for lager production. Actually it is normally an inferior malt to pale which is why the more complex decoction, two or three stage mashing process is employed. Like all the above malted barley grains it possesses the ability to mash other cereals.

Adjuncts

Now let's consider the adjuncts which must be mashed with diastatic extract or malt grain.

In my recipes I will only call for these to convert up to *a quarter of their weight* of added cereals. The limit has been decided on flavour and quality considerations rather than conversion ability. In theory some diastatic malt extracts and malt grain will deal with much more, but our home brew mashing techniques are not so precise and could cause problems with large cereal supplements.

Flaked Maize

The processed flakes of maize look like breakfast cereal cornflakes and are ready to use direct with diastatic malts. Raw cereals must be cooked and rolled as flakes to render them convertible.

Flaked maize is the most common adjunct and is particularly useful in Carlsberg style lagers to impart a "corn" flavour. Technically it can dilute the wort nitrogen and help to produce a clear, sparkling beer. When mashed it breaks down and yields the same balance of fermentable and unfermentable sugars as malted barley.

Flaked Rice

Choosing between flaked maize and rice depends on what part of the world the brewery is situated. Flaked rice has all the advantages of the corn but yields very little flavour. The neutral flavour is made full use of in delicate lagers in the American Budweiser vein. Our only source is from shops or supermarkets where it can be especially cheap if you can swing the cost onto the household budget! Home brew shops rarely sell it.

Flaked Barley

Barley flakes improve the head retention, body and flavour. Dark beers, such as Guinness, can tolerate a high proportion of this adjunct, but lighter coloured beers risk having their clarity marred through supended protein matter liberated from the flakes.

Torrefied Barley

A very large adjunct where the grain has been "puffed up" by heat treatment. It gives a nice nutty flavour and helps to make straining off easier after mashing. Unfortunately not often available.

Torrefied Wheat

An even more uncommon adjunct although the breakfast cereal "Puffed Wheat" makes an ideal substitute.

Wheat Malt

Wheat can be malted like barley, but not with the same degree of success. Belgian Lambric beers are sometimes brewed entirely from wheat malt and have a superb flavour, not really so different from traditional beer as I would have expected. Malted Wheat improves head retention as well as creating very interesting flavour changes.

Brewing Flour

Wheat flour, such as Brumore, is used extensively in British brewing practice. For our malt extract recipes it has the advantage of being totally convertible, leaving no debris to cause straining problems after mashing.

Rolled Oats

Rarely used nowadays due to the decline in oatmeal stouts. It tends to be a bit oily, which adversely affects the foam retention of the poured beer.

Breakfast Cereals

Quite a few breakfast cereals are ready to use direct in our brewing. Cornflakes (maize), Weetabix (wheat) and Krispies are often coated with malt extract for binding and flavouring. Normally they work out dearer than conventional adjuncts, but are ready at hand especially in times of emergency.

Requirements During Mashing

In the early days of home brewing, mashing gained a bad reputation for being a difficult, messy and unnecessary task. Unfortunately, much of this stigma has stuck. But really it is incredibly easy and a very desirable approach to home brewing producing a quality of beer rarely matched by other methods. Admittedly, the full "all malt grain" technique needs more consideration, but malt extract based mashing is well within the scope of every home brewer and not just an idealistic whim of the enthusiast.

Mashing is the traditional and easy way to brew: it was only home brewers who initially complicated the issue! If it was at all difficult, how on earth did the "ale wives" and brewers of yesteryear manage without the modern aids of electricity, gas, glass and plastic?

How the Reaction Works

The crushed grain is steeped in hot water to activate enzymes in the malt to initiate the chemical breakdown of starch into sugars of varying degrees of fermentability. At this stage, do not try to understand what enzymes *are*, but concentrate on what they *do*. It is easiest to explain the action of malt enzymes as being analogous to to the more tangible performance of yeast.

Yeast and diastase must have a liquid environment to work in. The temperature is very important. Too cold an environment will render yeast dormant. As the temperature rises, yeast activity increases and eventually becomes very vigorous. Because the conversion of sugar to alcohol takes days or weeks to complete, it is not desirable to hold the temperature to the pinnacle of maximum activity. This is because heat, whilst stimulating activity, also accelerates the death of the yeast cells. Putting figures to this reasoning, yeast starts working about 10°C. and gets killed off rapidly at temperatures over 50°C. To maintain a viable colony for the whole period of fermentation the brew should be kept at around 20°C.

Diastase follows a similar performance curve, but at a much higher temperature. Activity starts where the yeast would stop at around 50°C. The destruction of the amylase enzymes occurs rapidly over 70°C. However, because we want to create a swift reaction, over in an hour or so instead of days, we must conduct the mashing close to its destruction temperature. In practice the best temperature is around 65°C. (150°F.). The foregoing demonstrates that mashing can be conducted over a whole range of temperatures and is nowhere as restrictive as some earlier literature on home brewing suggested. Maintaining the mash between 60–67°C. virtually assures success.

Successful Mashing

The most critical stage in mashing is during the first ten minutes, where, if conditions are right, the majority of the starch conversion will have taken place. After this crucial period we can be more lax.

Assuming you follow the recipes in this book or other well designed formulation, failure to mash successfully is only likely on three counts. Firstly the reaction must take place in a slightly acidic environment, but following the recommended water treatments should obviate any problems on this score. Any doubt on the matter, test the mash with a slip of narrow range pH paper to ascertain if it lies between 5.0 and 6.0.

Secondly we must devise methods of mashing to minimise the risk of hot spots prematurely killing off the enzymes. In devising all my methods of mashing, the following objective is foremost in my mind.

TO MASH SUCCESSFULLY, KEEP THE TEMPERATURE AS CLOSE TO, BUT NOT EXCEEDING 66°C. (150°F.)— ESPECIALLY DURING THE FIRST TEN MINUTES OR SO.

More uncommon, but nevertheless possible, is a loss of diastatic power of the malt extract or grain. Age will decrease the enzyme activity and so can storage in the wrong conditions. Both sources should be kept in a reasonably cool place and be used up within six months of purchase.

When it Fails!

It is easy to check whether mashing has been successful by carrying out an Iodine Test (see page 44). However, if all the starch has not been converted within $1\frac{1}{2}$ hours then it is unlikely to be achieved as the mash stands. Supplementing the enzymes with fresh crushed pale malt grains or more diastatic malt extract (say $\frac{1}{2}$ lb.) may help and so would *diastase* enzyme powder. I would prefer to tackle the problem with these additions, but it does turn the mashing process into a bit of a marathon.

Another way is simply to accept the fact and carry on with the process. Technically the danger should be in risking a permanent starch haze in the finished beer. In practice I have not found this to be so.

My approach would be to strain off the offending grain with little or no washing out of extract. A loss of some extract will be experienced and the flavour will change slightly, but at least the brew has been saved. You will be amazed how good your "unsuccessful" brew turns out.

METHODS OF MASHING

Boiling Pan

Use about 1 pint of water for each pound of diastatic malt extract and grain (1 litre per kg.) and carry out any water treatment necessary.

Raise the temperature to around 55°C. and mix in the cold malt extract syrup. Stir *thoroughly* to ensure no smears of malt adhere to the pan bottom.

Sprinkle in the crushed or flaked adjuncts. Apply heat and stir *continuously* to ensure an even heat distribution. Monitor the progress and temperature rise with a thermometer. Raise the mixture up to 67°C. and switch off the heat. Keep the mash moving to absorb the latent heat from the surrounding metal work. Until you have got the measure of this technique it can be a wrist aching job, although you may take comfort that your effort has safeguarded the working life of the enzymes.

Now the problem is to minimise the effort in keeping the mash at 60–67°C. for another hour. In the first half hour continual stirring is advised every time heat is applied. Actually in practice it is no so arduous as it may seem on paper. The mash cools quite slowly really and I find the temperature want restoring only once or twice more.

I mash in an old saucepan and this can be placed in the oven after the first mixing has brought the temperature up to 67°C. Previously a heat run test must be conducted to determine the dial setting for keeping the oven between 60 and 67°C.

Iodine Test to Check for a Successful Mash

Mashing can only be regarded as successful when all the available starch in the grain has been converted to sugar. Normally, Starch End Point, as this stage is called, should be passed in 30 minutes.

To test, add a few drops of Iodine to a small sample removed from the mash tun. There should be no change from its natural brown colour. Any bluish-black discolouration indicates starch is still present and mashing should be prolonged. Discard tested sample and try later.

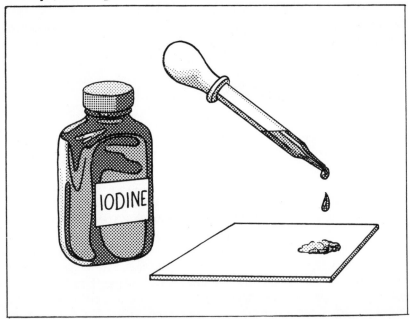

Mashing with the Bruheat

The Bruheat Boiler has a variable simmerstat capable of maintaining the mash at the right temperature. Accuracy of the temperature control depends on the fluid nature of the mash. Thick matting of grain around the element causes burning and erratic control. Consequently the grain content of the grist is best contained in one of the custom designed grain bags.

A typical malt extract mash would consist of diastatic malt syrup, often a measure of pale malt grains and some cereal flakes or flour. Adopt the following approach.

Add 2 gallons of water and any water treatment necessary. Switch on the heat and raise the temperature to around 45°C. The temperature is not critical at this stage. Measure out the required amount of diastatic malt syrup and pour in clear of the heating element. Stir efficiently to create an even mixture. Any brewing flour required must be creamed in cold water before being introduced to the malt solution. Raise the heat again, stirring continuously until the temperature reaches 65°C.

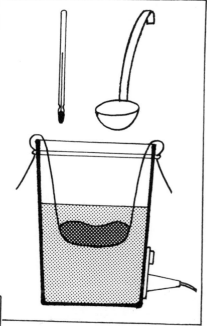

Turn back the dial and find the setting which makes the thermostat click "on" and "off" at this value. Automatic control is now set.

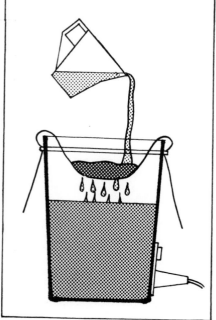

Raising the "grain" bag to drain and sparge the mashed grain.

The malt extract drains back into the Bruheat.

Position the grain bag into the liquid but above the level of the element and drape the top over the rim of the boiler. Secure with the elastic band provided.

Tip the grain malts and flakes into the bag and stir well in. Ensure the liquid level covers these. Mashing can now proceed without further attention except for an occasional check on the temperature. Because there is only a limited contact with the active enzymes in the malt solution, I stir the bag contents to coax a faster reaction.

As soon as mashing has been completed, pull the bag up out of solution and allow the extract from the mashed grains to drain back. Rinse with hot water to wash out any retained extract before discarding the redundant contents of the bag.

The mashed wort may now be boiled with the hops as normal.

Without a Bag

Some recipes call for the only minimum amount of grain and flakes. $\frac{1}{2}$ lb. (around 250 gm.) may be mashed successfully without being enclosed in a bag.

Warm the treated mashing water first. Stir in the malt syrup and dissolve thoroughly before mixing in the dry grist. As before, raise the mash temperature up to 65°C. and proceed under automatic control. Remember that a kitchen soup ladle is the best stirrer for floating the grain pieces evenly in the malt solution.

Using Mashing Immersion Heater

Combined immersion heater thermostats set around 65°C. (150°F.) may be used directly or indirectly to heat the mash. Either by suspending in the mixture or by maintaining the temperature of a water bath surrounding the mash tun.

Mix the mash initially up to 65°C. as recommended for the boiling pan method before transferring to the bucket. The heater needs positioning away from the plastic walls of the bucket before switching on.

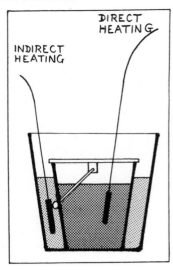

Sparging
(Washing the extract from the mashed grain.)

Tip the mashed grain into a grain straining bag supported over the boiler by a colander. Then gently jug hot water over the entire surface of the grain. Allow most of the washed out extract from each jug to be collected before sparging on some more.

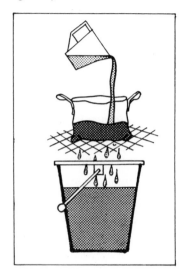

CASK BOND BITTER
A magnificent, traditional flavoured bitter.

5 gallons	Original Gravity 1044	25 litres
2 lb.	Diastatic Malt Extract	1 kg.
2 lb.	Crushed pale ale malt grains	1 kg.
4 oz.	Crushed crystal malt	125 gm.
2 oz.	Brewing flour	60 gm.
2 lb.	White sugar	1 kg.
1 lb.	Soft brown sugar	500 gm.
2 oz.	Fuggles hops	60 gm.
1 oz.	Goldings hops	30 gm.
	Beer yeast	

Pale ale salts containing gypsum are wanted here.

My traditional hops could be replaced with Northdown and Challenger if required. It is worth holding back some of the hops to late in the boil to improve flavour and aroma. Try to get the best yeast possible and preferably a commercial strain.

143

Method:

1. Put on 3½ pints (2 litres) of water to heat up to around 45°C. Cream the brewing flour and stir it in the water with the treatment salts.

2. Now add the malt extract and thoroughly dissolve before introducing the crushed grain quota. Using a soup ladle to keep the mash moving, raise the temperature up to 67°C. Mash between 60–67°C. for 1–1½ hours or until Starch End Point has passed.

3. Sparge into boiler, dissolve sugar, top up with cold water, add hops and boil for 1 hour. Strain into fermenting bin.

4. When cool add yeast and ferment until S.G. falls to 1008.

5. Rack off into gallon jars or polythene cube. Add beer finings and fit airlocks.

6. Allow the beer to settle for a few days before syphoning into primed bottles or cask.

7. Mature two weeks before drinking.

CAPTAIN'S STOUT

A rich distinctive brew.

3 gallons	Original Gravity 1039	15 litres
2 lb.	Diastatic malt syrup	1 kg.
8 oz.	Crushed pale malt	250 gm.
4 oz.	Crushed crystal malt	125 gm.
4 oz.	Flaked barley	125 gm.
6 oz.	Crushed black malt	200 gm.
2 lb.	White sugar	1 kg.
1½ oz.	Northern Brewer hops	45 g.
	Stout yeast	

Use mild ale water treatment as appropriate. An extra ½ teaspoon of common salt helps to round off this malty brew. A sweet version could be produced by adding 10 saccharins or similar during the fermentation.

Method:

Follow a similar procedure to the "Cask Bond Bitter" making allowances for the reduced quantity being brewed.

"OLD CONTEMPTIBLE"

A sparkling barley wine.

2 gallons	Original Gravity 1085/95	8.9 litres
3 lb.	Muntona Century malt extract	1½ kg.
8 oz.	Crushed wheat malt	250 gm.
2 teaspoon	Crushed black malt grains	10 ml.
2 lb.	Light soft brown sugar	1 kg.
3 oz.	Goldings hops	100 gm.
½ oz.	Northern brewer hops	15 gm.
	Wine yeast	

1. Mash the Century and crushed malts in water for 1 hour or until Starch End Point is passed.
2. Strain and sparge off extract and boil for 1 hour with the hops.
3. Strain off into another large saucepan or similar and dissolve in the sugar. Cool awhile and divide equally between two gallon jars.
4. Ferment with a wine yeast for 10 days under airlock. Rack off and top up to the neck with cold water and allow ferment to complete. The final gravity will be around 1012–18.
5. Bottle, priming with only ¼ teaspoon of sugar per pint.
6. Mature six months before drinking.

TRIDENT PALE ALE

A lusty, hoppy brew, strong and satisfying. Makes a good draught Pale Ale as well.

5 gallons	Original Gravity 1036	25 litres
4 lb.	Century malt extract	2 kg.
4 oz.	Flaked maize	125 gm.
4 oz.	Crushed wheat malt	125 gm.
2 lb.	Brewing sugar	1 kg.
1 teaspoon	Isomerised hop extract	5 ml.
2 oz.	Goldings hops	60 gm.
	Dried Beer yeast	

Pale Ale water treatment to be used as required. Irish Moss, yeast nutrient and heading salts are advised aids.

Method:

As per "Cask Bond" recipe except that the hop extract need not be boiled as part of the hop quota, but merely added with the sugar.

BISHOPS BROWN ALE

4 gallons	Original Gravity	20 litres
4 lb.	Diastatic malt extract	2 kg.
4 oz.	Flaked barley	125 gm.
8 oz.	Malto dextrin	250 gm.
4 oz.	Crushed chocolate malt	125 gm.
1 lb.	Glucose powder	500 gm.
2 oz. (equiv.)	Hop extract	60 gm. (equiv.)
	Dried beer yeast	

Follow "Cask Bond" recipe and boil extract in lieu of fresh hops.

MILLER MILD ALE

A quick maturing brew.

5 gallons	Original Gravity 1035	25 litres
3 lb.	Diastatic malt extract	$1\frac{1}{2}$ kg.
5 oz.	Flaked maize	150 gm.
3 teaspoon	Brewers caramel	15 ml.
2 lb.	White sugar	1 kg.
2 oz.	Northdown hops	60 gm.
	Dried beer yeast	

Method:
Basically the same as "Cask Bond" brew. Caramel is difficult to dispense accurately. It is best to dissolve more than you need in a little hot water in a separate saucepan then dose into the fermenting bin to get the right shade before the yeast is added.

SCOTCH ALE

5 gallons	Original Gravity 1038	25 litres
4 lb.	Diastatic malt syrup	2 kg.
1 lb.	Dark dried malt extract	500 gm.
6 oz.	Torrefied barley	200 gm.
1 lb.	Invert sugar	500 gm.
2 oz.	Fuggles hops	60 gm.
2 oz.	Northern brewer hops	60 gm.
	Dried beer yeast	

Include an extra $\frac{1}{2}$ teaspoon of Epsom Salts in the water treatment. Torrefied barley must be crushed in a coffee mill first. Flaked barley would be an acceptable alternative if it is difficult to get.

ALSTEIN LAGER

A light Pilsner brew.

5 gallons	Original Gravity 1032	25 litres
3 lb.	Century malt extract	1½ kg.
1 lb.	National malt extract	500 gm.
6 oz.	Flaked rice	200 gm.
2 oz.	Crushed wheat malt	60 gm.
1 lb.	Glucose chips	500 gm.
2 oz.	Hallertau hops	60 gm.
½ oz.	Styrian Golding hops	15 gm.
	Dried lager yeast	

Method:

As per "Cask Bond Bitter" recipe. Include the National extract quota in the hop boil instead of the mashing process. A stronger version can be brewed by only making 4 gallons from the above ingredients. The original gravity will be 1040 in this case.

TRIUMPH BITTER

A strong, full flavoured brew.

5 gallons	Original Gravity 1044	25 litres
3 lb.	Diastatic malt syrup	1½ kg.
3 lb.	Crushed pale malt	1½ kg.
5 oz.	Flaked maize	150 gm.
2 oz.	Flaked barley	60 gm.
1 lb.	Brown sugar	500 gm.
1 lb.	Golden syrup	500 gm.
2 oz.	Goldings hops	60 gm.
2 oz.	Hallertau hops	60 gm.
	Beer yeast	

Method:

As per "Cask Bond" brew.

GAZELLE LAGER

A clean sparkling lager.

5 gallons	Original Gravity 1044	25 litres
2 lb.	Diastatic malt extract	1 kg.
3 lb.	Crushed lager malt grains	1½ kg.
7 oz.	Flaked maize	225 gm.
2 lb.	White sugar	1 kg.
1½ oz.	Styrian Goldings hops	45 gm.
½ oz.	Goldings hops	15 gm.
	Lager yeast	

Method:

As per "Cask Bond" recipe, except this being a lager benefits from a few more weeks maturation.

CHAPTER 9

NORTH AMERICAN
HOME BREW PRACTICE

America is the largest producer of commercial beer and is destined to be the biggest home brew producer as well. Custom laws relating to the prohibition of home brewing are being relaxed or repealed throughout the continent bringing a welcomed and more enlightened attitude to the hobby.

American and Canadian amateur brewers can now enjoy much of the freedom and scope of their British colleagues. The home brew trade has backed their enthusiasm with an ever increasing range of products and ingredients. However, local malts, hops, sugars and yeast have different characteristics and demand a specialised approach to brew traditional North American beers.

In 1963 the restrictions on brewing wine and beer at home were lifted in Britain. It was the signal for success, and in ten years, home brewing became the country's leading leisure pastime enjoyed by millions of devotees to this new and satisfying hobby. President Carter signed the Beer and Wine Bill in late 1978, giving the same impetus to Americans and the right to any single person over 18 to brew 100 gallons of wine and beer a year legally and tax free. His signature on that document was like the first embryo yeast cell pitching into a waiting rich wort, ready to ferment, multiply and fire enthusiasm for the hobby.

America enjoys a style of beer of its own. Broadly classified as a lager beer, it is generally very much lighter in flavour and colour than Bavarian brews, and is chilled and carbonated more to accentuate its character.

It is easy to brew this style of beer at home. My techniques in the previous chapter are quite valid as most of the materials and equipment are available throughout North America. Employing malt extracts of British origin makes the brewing procedure easier, whereas the local versions give an edge on authentic flavour.

Canada uses the Imperial System of measurement the same as Britain, but the United States follow the same weight system but a smaller volume measurement, i.e.:

5 Imperial gallons = 6 U.S. gallons.

Readers in Britain can follow these recipes accepting that minor alterations may be necessary.

Nearly all beers call for the use of corn sugar, which is not generally available here, consequently, substitute these additions with invert sugar.

SIX PACK LAGER

Typical American beer; delicate, lightly flavoured and low enough in alcohol to be drunk in refreshing quantities. The recipe produces 5 gallons (U.S.) of beer around 3.4% alcohol.

Main Ingredients

2 lb.	**Malt extract syrup (D.M.S. or Light)**
1½ lb.	**Corn sugar**
1½ oz.	**Cascade hops**
	Dried lager yeast

Quality Aids

2 teaspoons yeast energiser—ensure healthy fermentation.

½–1 teaspoon citric acid—promotes speedy fermentation—use only ½ teaspoon with energiser.

1 teaspoon gypsum—improve hop flavour and beer clarity.

Gelatine finings—for clearing the beer after fermentation.

Heading agents—ensures lasting foam head.

Ascorbic acid—anti-oxidant desirable when "lagering" (storing) for a long time.

Sterilising agents—essential for brewing hygiene.

Main Brewing Equipment

Boiling pan—3 gallon minimum capacity.

Fermenting bin—6 gallon plastic bin with lid.

Hydrometer (beer tester)—for monitoring the brew's progress.

Secondary fermenter—5 gallon glass carboy or plastic poly container with airlock.

Bottles—dumpies or quarts with reseal caps.

Brewing Notes

Choose a light coloured malt extract. The dried powder extract could be used but the alcoholic strength will be slightly higher. Select whole fresh hops and a good quality yeast. Ready prepared water treatment may be substituted for the gypsum if convenient.

Instructions

1. Dissolve the malt extract and gypsum in as much water as practicable. Boiling pan to be no more than three quarters full.

2. Add 1 oz. of the hops and boil the mixture for 45 minutes. During the last 5 minutes boil add the remaining hops to inject and preserve flavour and aroma.

3. Strain off the clear wort from the redundant hop petals into a sterilised fermenting bin. Stir and dissolve in the corn sugar and top up to the 5 gallon mark with cold water.

4. Cool down to 20°C. (70°F.), add the yeast and energiser to start off the fermentation process. Loosely cover the brew with the lid or suitable cloth and ferment for 4–5 days. Skim off any brownish scum from the yeast head that forms. Stir the brew twice daily.

5. When fermentation comes to an end (as indicated by a hydrometer reading of around 1004 or 1B on your beer tester) syphon the brew into a sterilised secondary fermenter.

6. Store in a cool place for another week before adding the gelatine finings and ascorbic acid. Dissolve these agents in a little water first. Adequately disperse the mixture by stirring. The thin neck poses a bit of a problem which I overcome by using the "wrong end" (the long thin handle) of my brewers paddle.

7. The brew should now be left quietly in a cool place for **lagering**. One week is the minimum time, although the brew will benefit with maturation of up to two months under the right conditions.

8. When you are ready for bottling, prepare and sterilise 5 gallons worth of bottles, reseals and your primary fermentation vessel.

9. Syphon the brew into the primary fermenter and add the heading agent. Also dissolve one cup of corn sugar in a little hot water and stir this in as well. It is essential to take great care to disperse this priming sugar evenly to ensure that each bottle has the same amount and produces, by bottle fermentation, a safe and consistent gas pressure.

10. After mixing, syphon the brew into the bottles filling each one leaving $\frac{3}{4}$ inch airspace in "dumpies" and $1\frac{1}{2}$ inch in quarts.

11. Mature the brew for two weeks before sampling.

PITTSBURGH PILSNER

A full bodied lager.

6 U.S. gallons	Original Gravity 1050	25 litres
5 lb.	Light dried malt extract	2½ kg.
2 oz.	Crushed crystal malt	60 gm.
2 lb.	Corn sugar	1 kg.
2 oz.	Cascade hops	60 gm.
½ oz.	Hallertau or Saaz hops	15 gm.
	Dried lager yeast	

Follow basic method as demonstrated in "Six Pack" recipe. For the flavouring hops, Brewers Gold, Northern Brewer or Cluster could be substituted for the Cascade quota. I would only recommend using Saaz or English Goldings hops to replace the Hallertau though.

Again, yeast nutrient, gypsum, finings and heading agents are worthwhile. The latter could be omitted or reduced bearing in mind the high malt content of the brew. Boil the Cascade and half of the Hallertau hops for 45 minutes and pitch in the remainder for the last 5 minutes.

"SHOOT" LIGHT BEER

Ideal brew for everyday consumption.

6 U.S. gallons	Alcohol 3.5 per cent	25 litres
2½ lb.	Blue Ribbon hopped malt extract	1¼ kgm.
1 lb.	Light malt extract	500 gm.
¼ oz.	Cascade hop pellets	10 gm.
1 lb.	Corn syrup	500 gm.
	Dried lager yeast	

Follow "Six Pack" recipe except add the hopped malt extract after the boil and only boil the light variety with the pellets. Also put 6 saccharin tablets to the secondary fermentation vessel to smooth the flavour.

CARLTON CREAM ALE

5 U.S. gallons	Original Gravity 1049	20 litres
2½ lb.	Dark malt extract	1¼ kgm.
2 lb.	D.M.S. or light extract	1 kg.
2 lb.	Corn sugar	1 kg.
1 oz.	Flavour hops (Talisman, Cluster Brewers Gold)	30 gm.
1 oz.	Aroma hops (Cascade, Saaz)	30 gm.
	U.S. Ale yeast	

Follow basic "Six Pack" recipe. Substitute 1 teaspoon of non-iodized salt for the gypsum. Save ½ oz. of the aroma hops for the last 5 minutes boil.

MEDALLION MALT LIQUOR

A mashing recipe for that true traditional flavour.

5 U.S. gallons	Original Gravity 1004	20 litres
2 lb.	D.M.S. malt extract	1 kg.
3 lb.	Crushed pale malt grains	1½ kg.
4 oz.	Flaked maize	125 gm.
2 lb.	Corn sugar	1 kg.
1 oz.	Cascade hop pellets	30 gm.
	Dried U.S. ale yeast	

Brewing Notes

Mashing requires that little bit more attention by the brewer. Full guidance is given in Chapter 8 to clarify any doubts. However for this particular brew, dissolve the malt extract in 2 gallons of hot tap water (around 40°C.). Add 1 teaspoon gypsum and 1 teaspoon of lactic or citric acid and stir in the crushed grains and flakes. Using a thermometer, monitor the temperature and raise it to 67°C. Maintain this temperature as close to but not exceeding this value for 1–1½ hours. Strain off through a large sieve or cheesecloth and wash out the absorbed extract with hot water. Crumble the hop pellets into the wort and boil for at least 1 hour and preferably 2. Make up evaporated liquid if the solution becomes too thick.

Strain off the boiled wort into a sterilised fermenting bin.

From now proceed with the fermentation and bottling as per the "Six Pack" recipe.

OLD SIOUX

A high gravity strong ale that commands respect. Best described as an American Bavarian Barley Wine!

3 U.S. gallons	Original Gravity 1080	12 litres
3 lb.	Light dried malt extract	1½ kg.
2 lb.	Crushed lager malt grains	1 kg.
4 oz.	Crushed crystal malt grains	125 gm.
2 lb.	Corn sugar	1 kg.
½ lb.	Golden brown Barbados sugar	250 gm.
1½ oz.	Hallertau hops	45 gm.
1½ oz.	Saaz hops	45 gm.
	Wine yeast	

Brewing Notes

Mash the malt grains as per the Malt Liquor recipe. Boil all the hops with the wort for 1 hour. Dissolve in the corn and brown sugar and adjust the volume to 3 gallons after straining off. Ferment with a wine yeast (necessary for high alcohol tolerance) for 10–14 days. Rack off into gallon jars fitted with airlocks and leave until the fermentation ceases. Normally this should take 1–2 months at *normal* room temperature. Rack off sediment and return to the gallon jars and let the beer mature for another month before bottling.

Prime each gallon with ½ oz. of sugar in solution before bottling. Mature for at least 1 month before drinking.

"CRUSHER" STEAM BEER

Steam beer is about the only traditional style American beer still brewed commercially. An excellent naturally conditioned brew produced without resorting to expensive refrigeration equipment. It is best fermented around 15°C., but even at normal room temperature, 20°C., the results are good so long as a high quality bottom fermenting yeast is used. I found a wine yeast worked well on this recipe. The expression "steam" refers to the lively foam and fobbing when the brew is dispensed from its draught container. A home brew pressure barrel or stainless steel keg are ideal for storing and serving this brew properly.

As with many American beers, steam beer should be an all malt formulation. However, because of the flavour taints imparted in malt extracts by the concentration process, a beer made entirely of malt extract is cloying and not true to character.

6 U.S. gallons	Original Gravity 1039	25 litres
2 lb.	Edme D.M.S. malt extract	1 kg.
4 lb.	Crushed pale malt grains	2 kg.
3 oz.	Crushed crystal malt grains	100 gm.
8 oz.	Flaked rice	250 gm.
1 lb.	Cane sugar	500 gm.
2 oz.	Flavour hops (Northern Brewer, Brewers Gold, Cluster)	60 gm.
1 oz.	Aroma hops (Hallertau, Cascade, Saaz)	30 gm.
	Lager or wine yeast	

Brewing Notes

Mash the malt extract, malt grains and flakes as per "Medallion Malt Liquor" recipe. Boil the mashed extract with the hops remembering to save a portion of the aroma hops for the last 5 minutes boil. Aroma hops as pellets or powder in sealed sachets keep particularly fresh and are worth saving for such a fine brew as this.

Add the sugar to the strained off hopped wort and make up to 6 gallons with cold water. Add yeast and nutrient and ferment six days in the primary fermentation vessel and three weeks in the secondary vessel. Add gelatine finings during the latter stage.

Cask the beer in a barrel and prime with one cup of cane sugar and heading liquid. To get barrel conditioning off to a good start "Krausen" the beer by pouring in a bottle of like home brew, sediment and all.

Check condition and flavour after a weeks maturation.

INDEX